THE Commands OF Christ

Unlocking God's Plan for Effective Discipleship

Todd Brown & Stacey Burkholder

Copyright © 2024 by Todd Brown and Stacey Burkholder
First Paperback Edition

All rights reserved. No part of this publication may be reproduced, distributed, or transmitted in any form or by any means, including photocopying, recording, or other electronic or mechanical methods, without the prior written permission of the publisher, except in the case of brief quotations embodied in critical reviews and certain other noncommercial uses permitted by copyright law. For permission requests, write to the publisher, addressed "Attention: Permissions Coordinator," at the address below.

Bible versions used:

Unless otherwise noted, Scriptures are taken from the Holy Bible, New International Version®, NIV® Copyright © 1973, 1978, 1984, 2011 by Biblica, Inc.® Used by permission. All rights reserved worldwide

The Holy Bible, English Standard Version. ESV® Text Edition: 2016. Copyright © 2001 by Crossway Bibles, a publishing ministry of Good News Publishers.

New King James Version® (NKJV). Copyright © 1982 by Thomas Nelson. Used by permission. All rights reserved.

Holy Bible, New Living Translation (NLT). Copyright © 1996, 2004, 2015 by Tyndale House Foundation. Used by permission of Tyndale House Publishers, Inc., Carol Stream, Illinois 60188. All rights reserved.

Some names, businesses, places, events, locales, incidents, and identifying details inside this book have been changed to protect the privacy of individuals.

Published by Freiling Agency, LLC.

P.O. Box 1264
Warrenton, VA 20188

www.FreilingAgency.com

PB ISBN: 978-1-963701-86-9
E-book ISBN: 978-1-963701-10-4

Table of Contents

Acknowledgments v
Foreword vii
Introduction ix

SECTION 1: THE MARKS OF A DISCIPLE

1	Love One Another	3
2	You Must Be Born Again	7
3	Believe in Me	11
4	Repent	15
5	Take Up Your Cross	19
6	Love Me	23
7	Worship the Father	27

SECTION 2: INTIMACY WITH THE FATHER

8	Come to Me	33
9	Remain in Me	37
10	Hear My Words	41
11	Always Pray and Never Give Up	45
12	Practice Secrecy	49
13	Do the Will of My Father	55
14	Be Ready. Watch and Wait	61

SECTION 3: THE HARD STUFF

15	Fear Him Who Can Destroy Both Body and Soul	67
16	Enter Through the Narrow Door	71
17	Do Not Lust	75
18	Render Unto Caesar	79
19	Your Righteousness Must Exceed That of the Pharisees	83

| 20 | Be Perfect | 87 |
| 21 | Endure Patiently | 91 |

SECTION 4: RELATIONSHIPS

22	Become a Servant	99
23	What God Has Joined Together, Let No Man Separate	103
24	Honor Your Parents	109
25	Love Your Neighbor As Yourself	113
26	Do Unto Others	119
27	Forgive	123
28	Go and Be Reconciled	127

SECTION 5: MINDSET

29	Store Up Treasures in Heaven	133
30	Beware of Covetness	137
31	Do Not Worry	141
32	Do Not Be Afraid	145
33	Ask, Seek, Knock	149
34	Rejoice and Be Glad	155
35	Remember Me	159

SECTION 6: SHARING THE GOOD NEWS

36	Let Your Light Shine	167
37	Invite the Poor	171
38	Let the Children Come	177
39	Do Not Judge	181
40	Go the Second Mile	187
41	Love Your Enemies	193
42	Pray for Workers	199

Conclusion
    Keep My Commandments 205
Endnotes 211

Acknowledgments

When Stacey Burkholder and I planned a yearlong series on the commands of Jesus, we prepared Sunday-morning sermons, not a book. Turning nearly 50 messages into a manuscript was a daunting and time-consuming task. Without the help of some special people, it would never have happened. I want to acknowledge two people who did that hard work and saw this book through to completion.

Anita Wood has been my friend and partner in ministry for nearly thirty years. On top of her work as my administrative assistant in a very busy church, she transcribed all of these sermons—from video to the initial manuscript—making important editorial changes in the process.

Amber Parker is one of the busiest Christians I know. She is in leadership at a wonderful ministry, Advancing Native Missions, active in the church here, and an author and conference speaker. Amber condensed these sermons into chapters, organized them into meaningful sections, and added her own insights along the way. She maneuvered us through the book writing and publishing process in a way we would not have done as easily without her.

On behalf of Stacey, the Bridge Elders and staff, and a congregation that will use this book as a teaching tool for years to come, we're all very grateful to Anita and Amber for this labor of love.

—**Pastor Todd Brown**
September 12, 2024

Foreword

Throughout my life, I have enrolled in many discipleship programs. I checked all the prescribed boxes: scripture memorization, prayer, and witnessing. All good but lacking. Finally, during one week-long Christian training program, I discovered where true Christian joy comes from.

Have you wondered what the key to authentic Christian living is? Maybe, like me, you have searched for it in programs, experiences, or in your own effort. You may be starting to feel weary of it all. You may even be thinking that Christian joy is unattainable. And then, here in this book, Todd Brown and Stacey Burkholder propose that the key to Christian living is hiding in plain sight, right in front of us. They suggest that the key is found in following Christ's commands.

How well do you know Christ's commands? There's "Love one another." – That's a great idea! Or "Make disciples of all nations." – Great! Let's send missionaries. And then there's "Be perfect" – Huh, what? "Forgive seventy times seven." Did Jesus really mean that? Far too often, we dismiss the importance of knowing and obeying Christ's commands.

At a time when our culture is unraveling, it is vital that the Church act like the Church. The Church Jesus died for. The Church He left on earth to be an example of His love and joy. This book you hold in your hands is the handbook to get you not into a program but into a lifestyle of joy. In it, you will discover the key to true authentic Christian living. Is it easy? No. Don't expect easy. Instead, expect to meet Jesus in a whole new way, deepen your walk with Him, and enjoy greater fellowship with those on the same journey.

This book is not just theory. It has been put into practice. My children and six of my grandchildren attend Bridge Christian Church, where Todd and Stacey pastor. I have personally known Todd for many years. We have worked together at an event for persecuted Christians and have prayed together for persecuted Christians worldwide. I have observed his heart for people and discipleship up close. While I haven't had the privilege to get to know Stacey as well, my family testifies he has this same heartbeat. I have also seen the discipleship of my grandchildren. They have grown in their faith and love for Jesus and His Word. I am deeply grateful for how they have been nurtured in their faith and witness. They take Jesus seriously.

Todd and Stacey have given us this simple, practical, and profound book. It is an important book for the Church today. I pray it will find its way into the hands of every Christ-follower.

—**Ruth Graham**
Author of *Transforming Loneliness, Deepening Our Relationships With God And Others When We Feel Alone*

Introduction

So, the final test of love is obedience. Not sweet emotions, not willingness to sacrifice, not zeal, but obedience to the commandments of Christ.
— A.W. Tozer

I remember reading an Edgar Allen Poe story in high school called "The Purloined Letter". The plot reveals the Queen of France losing a correspondence whose contents, if broadcast, would bring her shame and embarrassment. When brought in to find the letter, the French police uncovered that someone in the queen's court had stolen the letter, but they had no way to prove it.

Convinced the thief would have a special hiding place, they tore his house apart, searching everywhere, to no avail. Desperate, they called in Detective C. Auguste Dupin. Within an hour, Dupin found the letter. And do you know where the letter was? It was laid out in plain sight. The thief knew his home would be searched intently, so he left it out in the open, hoping it would be overlooked.

We often miss seeing what is right in front of us, those things hiding in plain sight. This applies when we can't find the milk in the fridge or the shirt in our closet and to much more important things. If you are reading this book, chances are you want to grow as a disciple of Christ. You want to learn how to live out your faith and make an impact in the world. But for many of us, finding the *way* to grow can feel like an endless and frustrating search for hidden treasure.

Every church I've ever been involved in is searching for how to make effective disciples. We've tried small groups, different books, different courses. We've signed people up for six weeks of this or twelve weeks of that. But what if the quest to follow Jesus is not as complicated as we make it? What if the answer to real spiritual growth is "hiding in plain sight," laid out right on the pages of Scripture?

Most of you are familiar with the Great Commission. After His crucifixion, Jesus is alive, resurrected from the dead in a new body. Before He ascends into Heaven back to His Father, He gathers His disciples on a mountain and gives them instructions. These instructions are particular. He's not just saying goodbye; He is training them, teaching them how to make disciples effectively.

"Then Jesus came to them and said, 'All authority in Heaven and on earth has been given to me. Therefore, go and make disciples of all nations, baptizing them in the name of the Father and of the Son and of the Holy Spirit, and teaching them to obey everything I have commanded you. And surely, I am with you always, to the very end of the age'" (Matthew 28:18-20).

Jesus instructs His followers that **effective disciple-making is teaching baptized believers to identify His commands and train them to obey those commands.** It is these commands that became "the Apostles' doctrine" that the church in Acts 2 devoted themselves to and lived by. As a result, the early church flourished and more new believers joined the church every day (Acts 2:47).

I believe that the search for an effective discipleship program in the modern church has not been found because we've opted for other measures than the Great Commission. Often these words of Christ are relegated to "marching orders" for missionaries rather than the clear and simple solution for steadily raising up mature Christians in the church.

I'll be honest with you: I grew up in the church, my dad was a pastor, I went to Bible college, and I've been in the ministry for years. Yet I had never spent time trying to identify the commands of Jesus, let alone intentionally, systematically, thoroughly, teach or preach them. Like most pastors, I was always on the hunt for *another* effective discipleship program when the authoritative plan of Jesus was right there in front of me, hiding in plain sight.

So, in our 28th year as a church, Bridge Christian Church did something unlike anything we had ever done. Unlike anything I've ever participated in. We decided to spend the entire year on one series we called *Red Letters, the King's Commands.* Pastor Stacey Burkholder and I identified over 40 commands of Jesus, given to us in the four Gospels and the Book of Revelation. Then we committed to an intentional, systematic, thorough way of teaching these commands week-by-week to help our church know and obey these commands. This book contains some of what we taught and learned on that journey.

Introduction

These commands of Jesus are not suggestions, guidelines, or mantras. They were spoken with authority by the Son of God. While Jesus walked humbly on this earth as a man, He still was the King of Kings and Lord of Lords, reigning forever (Revelation 17:14). His commands are authoritative, the words of the King given to His people. As His followers, we need to know these commands and commit to putting them into practice. This is the "secret" to effective discipleship, laid out for us in "plain sight".

My hope and prayer are that you will do just that, make a commitment to study the commands of Jesus and put them into practice. I am confident if you do, your life and your church will be transformed.

—**Pastor Todd Brown**

SECTION 1

THE MARKS OF A DISCIPLE

Jesus said, "If you hold to my teaching, you are really my disciples. Then you will know the truth, and the truth will set you free."

John 8:31-32

CHAPTER 1

LOVE ONE ANOTHER

> *The divine strategy by which the Lord intends to bring the world to an awareness of Jesus Christ is to create in the midst of the world, a family. A family life, a shared life so that men and women all over the earth becoming by new birth, members of that life, enter into a family circle which is so unmistakable and so filled with joy and warmth that the world observing it will envy it.* —Ray Stedman

The word *gospel* literally means a good telling or a good story. The four Gospels, written by and named for Matthew, Mark, Luke, and John, contain the "good telling" of Jesus Christ. These books record the life, miracles, and teachings of Jesus. It is from the four Gospels we find the commands of Jesus.

Through studying church history, we learn that John lived far longer than all the other disciples until around age 90. One historical account reveals that in the last years of John's life, when his movement and speech were limited, he would still address the church. In order to do so, two men would get on either side of his chair, lift him, bring him to the front, and place him there. Once situated, John would look out at the people, and all he could do was repeat these words; "Little children love each other." John's life, leadership, and experience could be narrowed down to the greatest thing: Love one another as Christ has loved you.

If we look toward the end of John's Gospel account, we find Jesus giving this most important command that marks the life of all of His disciples. After three and a half years of leading His disciples as their rabbi and teacher, Jesus brought them to Jerusalem, the capital city of Israel, where He would soon be crucified. He gathers them together in an upper room to observe the Jewish feast of Passover, knowing that by the next day, His body will be buried in the grave.

During this Passover meal, Jesus will wash the disciples' feet. He will point out His betrayer, and He will rightly predict that they will all desert Him. He will even speak directly to Peter, "that before sunup you will deny three times you even know me" (Luke 22:34). Imagine the melancholy pall that settled into that upper room with this disturbing prediction.

It is in the middle of that meal and foreboding news that Jesus announces something startling:

> **"A new command I give you: Love one another. As I have loved you, so you must love one another. By this everyone will know that you are my disciples, if you love one another."**
> **John 13:34**

After issuing many commands in their journey together, this is nearly the last command Jesus gives His disciples. It seems He saved the most important command for the end, making sure they didn't miss it: *Love each other in the manner I have loved you.*

The disciples had seen Jesus's love and compassion issued to thousands of people. They'd heard Him speak tenderly to a woman caught in adultery. They'd seen Him, in love, touch the blind, the lame, the diseased. They'd personally received comforting words of love and affection from their Master. He washed their feet. And soon, they would see the full extent of His love for them when He would die on a cross for their sins.

In John 15, John records as Jesus continued teaching on the topic of love. Allow me (Todd) to paraphrase these precious last words of our Savior. *I've loved you in the very same way my Father has loved me. Remain in my love by obeying what I command, just like I obey my Father. Let me say it again. Love each other as I have loved you and live a life of extravagant love, great love, the greatest of loves, by laying down your life for someone else. Jesus continues, and now, one more time, one last time, are you listening? I command you to love each other.*

Notice that Jesus doesn't mince words; He doesn't say *I really would appreciate it if you'd follow my suggestion to love each other*. There's no option; there's no wiggle room. This is a command. And most of us have reduced this command by half. Jesus is telling us to do much more than love each other. He commands us to love others in the same way He has loved us.

Consider this familiar verse and the extent of Jesus's love. "For God so loved the world that he gave his only begotten Son that whoever would believe in him would not perish but have eternal life" (John 3:16).

For God so loved the world that He gave—out of His flock, a lamb without blemish, His only Son. Jesus is talking about loving one another in the same fashion that He loved us by dying on the cross. There is no greater love than that kind of love.

Let's go to the scene at the foot of the cross for a minute. Jesus was impaled by the Romans, hands and feet spread out, naked, bleeding to death in horrible agony, and John was the only disciple present. Standing right there, seeing his rabbi writhing in pain, I've got to wonder if, in the middle of the shouting and jeering and panic and pain, something was happening in John's heart and he was beginning to realize, *this is what you've been talking about. This is the great love you're expressing; this is what you're calling me to; this is how you want us to love.*

We know something did indeed happen in John's heart and mind because love became the theme of his life. If you turn to the back end of the New Testament, you'll see three little letters he wrote repeating over and over this theme: If we claim to know Jesus, we must follow His command to love.

This command teaches us that in the body of Christ, in the church of our Lord, among brothers and sisters, this family, there's no room for hate. There is no room for jealousy, slander, gossip, or meanness. Listen to John, not me. Listen to what he said: If you claim to love God, if you claim to be a follower, a disciple of Jesus, you must remember that we are called to love each other, as Christ has loved us, not only on our best days but our worst. If you allow these resentments toward others, these resentments you hold on to or cling to or even cherish, your faith is a fraud, and you are a liar.

When we read the opening chapters of the Book of Acts, we see that the early church exemplified Christ's love to one another. The great love between brothers and sisters blossomed into something brand new, and thousands of people were attracted, not only to the Gospel message but to this loving relationship with each other. Many came knocking on the doors of that early church wanting to be a part.

Consider the church of today. What does the world think about us? Are we loving each other with the kind of sacrificial love Christ showed us? Are those outside pressing their noses up against our windows, knocking on our doors wanting to come in? Or are they running the other direction, because what they've seen is meanness, jealousy, cliques, and hypocrisy?

Let's learn from John's example and allow our lives to be focused on learning how to live out Jesus's command to love one another. When we do, we have the power to change the world.

Read: John 15:9-17, 1 John 2:3-6, 1 John 3:16, 23-24, 1 John 4:20; 2 John 6

Reflect: What is the extent of Jesus's love for me? Am I loving others with that same love?

Pray: God, help me to understand the depths of Your love for me. Teach me to love others with that same love. Help me see those around me with compassion and kindness. Show me how to put Your love into action today.

CHAPTER 2

You Must Be Born Again

Many Christians have the mistaken notion that eternal life begins when they die. But that is not biblically accurate. Eternal life begins when we are born again into the Kingdom of God.
—David Jeremiah

Jesus made a lot of shocking statements. Of the most shocking were His claims to be the Son of God. Imagine the people around Him trying to grasp how this thirty-year-old retired carpenter could be the Messiah. Most religious leaders rejected Jesus's claims, but not all of them. John Chapter 3 records an encounter between Jesus and Nicodemus, one of the Pharisees. We don't know exactly what drew Nicodemus in—maybe something in Jesus's teaching or the miracles He performed—but under cover of night, Nicodemus came to find out more.

Nicodemus begins the conversation by saying, "We know you are a teacher from God; no one else could do the things you are doing; you are a great miracle worker." It seems it's on the tip of his tongue; he's about to ask, are you the Messiah? Are you the Promised One? But Jesus takes their conversation in a different direction with His response.

> **"Jesus replied, 'Very truly I tell you, no one can see the kingdom of God unless they are born again.'"**   **John 3:3**

Nicodemus is caught off guard, and he's confused. He responds, "How could this be?" When Jesus spoke of being born again, He used the Greek word *genao*, meaning physical birth, to bring out offspring from procreation. Nicodemus doesn't understand how a man can be born more than once. It is not like a person can re-enter their mother's womb for a second time.

Jesus patiently explains He is talking about spiritual birth: "The flesh gives birth to flesh, but the Spirit gives birth to spirit. You should not be surprised at my saying; you must be born again. The wind blows wherever it pleases. You hear its sound, but you cannot tell where it comes from or where it is going. So it is with everyone born of the Spirit" (John 3:7-8).

Even with this explanation, Nicodemus again asks how these things can be. Maybe later, as he replays the conversation, he remembers the words of the prophet Ezekiel, who wrote about the coming Savior, the Messiah: "I will sprinkle clean water on you, and you will be clean; I will cleanse you from all your impurities and from all your idols. I will give you a new heart and put a new spirit in you; I will remove from you your heart of stone and give you a heart of flesh. I will put my Spirit in you and move you to follow my decrees and be careful to keep my laws" (Ezekiel 36:25-27).

Ezekiel understood the coming Savior would redeem His people through washing and rebirth. For centuries, the Jewish people, including Nicodemus, had practiced a ceremonial bathing called *mikveh*. *Mikveh* is a bath, a ceremony, a religious bathing in the presence of a priest. The man or woman would remove their old clothes and put on a white robe. Sometimes, they would plunge naked beneath the waters of *mikveh*, as in the Old Testament times.

Most often, *mikveh* was used as a predicate for someone getting married. The groom or bride, or sometimes together, would perform *mikveh*, plunging beneath the waters to prepare themselves for their marriage. With this ceremony, they were saying, "I'm done with my old lovers, I'm done with my old way of life, I'm done with my past, we want to come together in this new relationship, pure and clean before God." And from *mikveh*, they would put their wedding clothes on and go on to their ceremony.[1]

When John the Baptist was baptizing in the wilderness, it was before the Christian baptism we practice today began. This purely Jewish ceremonial cleansing was actually *mikveh*, signaling that the participant was repentant of sin and desired forgiveness and a new start.

The Apostle Paul wrote about the new birth, this idea of being born again, and regeneration in Romans 6:4: "We were buried therefore with him by baptism into death, in order that, just as Christ was raised from the dead by the glory of the Father, we too might walk in newness of life."

Paul Washer observes, "In modern day evangelism, this precious doctrine (of regeneration) has been reduced to nothing more than a human decision to raise one's hand, walk an aisle, or pray a sinner's prayer. As a result, the majority of Americans believe that they've been 'born again' even though their thoughts, words, and deeds are a continual contradiction to the nature and will of God."[2]

What about you? Are you walking in the "newness of life"?

Several years ago, I (Todd) had a conversation with a waitress at Shoney's. She had been a hard worker all of her life and had worked for the last twenty years at Shoney's. As I got to know her, I asked her, "What is the toughest part of your job?" I expected her to say something like the wear and tear on her legs, but instead, she said, "The toughest part of my job is Sunday when church lets out." "Why?" I asked. "Well, that's when all the born-again Christians come to eat, and they can be some of the rudest customers we see. I'm amazed how rude they can be, the language they use, and many waitresses where I work don't want anything to do with the church because of that."

What about you? What's your life outside of church look like?

Listen to what Paul writes: "Don't you know that wrongdoers will not inherit the Kingdom of God, don't be deceived. And that is what some of you were. But you were washed, you were sanctified, you were justified in the name of the Lord Jesus Christ and by the Spirit of our God" (I Corinthians 6:11).

Jesus is clear: The promise of the Kingdom of God is only for those who have been born again. If we have truly been born again, we should rejoice together that our eternity has already begun. Prone to sin, yes; weak in body and spirit, yes. But one day, we will have a new body, a new life forever.

In Hebrews, we find a passage that echoes the words of Ezekiel: "Let us draw near to God with a sincere heart and with the full assurance that faith brings, having our hearts sprinkled to cleanse us from a guilty conscience and having our bodies washed with pure water" (Hebrews 10:22).

One of the reasons we are obedient to Jesus's command to baptize disciples is because baptism, what I would call Christian *mikveh*, contains within it the very promise of Ezekiel, the words of Jesus, and the teachings of the apostles. We bring ourselves to meet God by faith. We are cleansed and filled with His Spirit. And we look forward to the day we will be present with Him in the Kingdom of Heaven.

Read: 1 Peter 1:3-4, 24, Romans 6:4, 2 Corinthians 5:17, Acts 2:37-41, Titus 3:3-6

Reflect: Have I been born again? Does my life reflect my new birth?

Pray: Thank You for the gift of new life. Teach me how to fully walk in the newness of life. Show me any ways I am falling short of Your calling.

CHAPTER 3

BELIEVE IN ME

Mankind must believe in Jesus because we are in a desperate situation, and only he can rescue us. It's like a fireman carrying someone from a burning building who cannot save themselves.
—*John Piper*

Belief is a distinguishing mark of the disciples of Jesus. A quick word study reveals that Matthew, Mark, and Luke used the word "believe" thirty-four times combined, while in John's Gospel alone, we find the word eighty-four times.

> **"Do not let your hearts be troubled. You believe in God; believe also in me." John 14:1**

John uses the action of belief to distinguish those turning to Jesus and those turning away from Jesus. In John 12:37, John describes one group of people who saw many signs: "They still would not believe in him." Then, in verse 42, he describes another group: "Many, even among the leaders, believe in him."

What is behind the word "believe"? It is much more than our common expressions of "I believe in you" or "believe in yourself." John understood that Jesus's call to believe was a remedy for sin, the rescue from God's wrath and judgment.

In John 8, we find Jesus in a conflict with the religious leaders. Jesus makes an interesting statement that results in many believing in Him, "When you have lifted up the Son of Man, then you will know that I am he and that I do nothing on my own but speak just what the Father has taught me. The one who sent me is with me; he has not left me alone, for I always do what pleases him.' Even as he spoke, many believed in him" (John 8:28-30).

During Jesus's encounter with Nicodemus, He makes a similar reference to being lifted up: "Just as Moses lifted up the snake in the wilderness, so the Son of Man must be lifted up, that everyone who believes may have eternal life in him" (John 3:14-15).

Jesus's strange language points us to a strange Old Testament story recorded in Numbers 20-21. Here, we find the children of Israel, after being rescued from slavery, journeying in the wilderness. Theologians predicted that there could have been two million people living in tents, moving through the wilderness, a huge number of people with their flocks and herds with them. These people are described as "stiff-necked and rebellious" and as "grumblers." They complained about pretty much everything— the water, the food, the heat. They even went as far as to say, "It would be better for us to go back to Egypt and be slaves again to Pharoah!"

Can you imagine? Because of their grumbling, God sent an awful plague, a plague of poisonous snakes. Hideous snakes began biting people, and people everywhere were dying from the snake bites. They were experiencing a plague caused by their rebellion and their sin.

The leaders of Israel found Moses and begged him to pray for them so they could be saved. Moses went into his quiet place and prayed for the people's salvation. God responded with bizarre instructions to fashion a snake from bronze, put it on a pole, and put it up in the middle of the camp. Then anyone who looked up to the bronze snake would be healed. Moses obeyed, the people of Israel looked up for healing, and the plague stopped.

This Old Testament story points to our need for salvation. We are living in a generation that doesn't know God. More and more are turning their backs on God, His church, and His people. We are not very different from the generation in Noah's day when God destroyed the world with a great flood. "The Lord saw how great the wickedness of the human race had become on the earth, and that every inclination of the thoughts of the human heart was only evil all the time" (Genesis 6:5).

All of us have been snake-bitten by sin. The venom of sin and death courses through us all, and the only antidote is belief in Jesus. Jesus knew His purpose: to bring salvation. He would be lifted up on a cross. He who had no sin became sin so that we could be saved.

Believing is more than just acknowledging that Jesus existed and believing the Bible is true. In James 2, James warns the first-century church that even the demons believe in God and shudder. If our belief doesn't move from our head to our heart, it is not saving belief; it is not faith.

When we truly believe in Jesus, life-changing actions are set in motion. As I (Todd) talk to children about following Jesus, I often have them trace their hands on a piece of paper. Each finger helps them remember one word about what it means to be a disciple of Jesus. Each word, when lived out, flows into the next. Here is what I help them learn:

1. **Belief:** You must believe, not just in your head but in your heart, the kind of belief that grips you and convicts you and spurs in you what's next.

2. **Repentance:** Repentance literally means turning away from the direction you've been going and starting to go another way; a change of heart and attitude. It is an awareness of and sorrow for the sin in your life.

3. **Confession:** The confession of faith publicly says *I believe that Jesus is the Christ, the Son of the living God.* You speak it the day you give your heart to Jesus, and it should be on your lips each day forward in your school, in your place of business, everywhere you go.

4. **Christian baptism:** Baptism says, *I am all in, and I want the world to know that I am all in.* Through baptism, we are buried with Christ in the likeness of His death so that we can be raised with Christ in the likeness of His resurrection.

5. **Steadfastness:** Perseverance is the mark of a believer. It declares, *I'm never going back, I'm never giving in. I may stumble along the way, but I am committed to the arduous journey with Christ.*

Listen to the writer of Hebrews exhorting the church in his day. "See to it, brothers and sisters, that none of you has a sinful, unbelieving heart that turns away from the living God. But encourage one another daily, as long as it is called, "today," so that none of you may be hardened by sin's deceitfulness. We have come to share in Christ, if indeed we hold our original conviction firmly to the very end" (Hebrews 3:12-14).

Are you faltering in your belief today? Are you wavering in your commitment to Jesus? Jesus is saying to you, *stay firm to the end. Believe in Me.*

Read: John 3:36, John 5:24, John 8:24, I Corinthians 15:1-2

Reflect: What impact has believing in Jesus made in your life? Are there any areas you are struggling with unbelief?

Pray: God, thank You for providing me with a rescue from sin. Like the people of Israel who looked to the bronze serpent for healing, I look to You for spiritual healing. Jesus, I believe in You.

CHAPTER 4

REPENT

Today's church has the misconception that we can add Christ to our lives but not subtract sin. It's a change in belief without a change in behavior; it longs for revival without repentance.
—*Patrick Morley*

Do you know what the topic of Jesus's first recorded sermon was? It was not forgiveness, do unto others, or even love. Matthew tells us from the beginning of His public ministry, out of the gate, Jesus preached repentance.

> **"From that time on Jesus began to preach, 'Repent, for the kingdom of Heaven has come near.'"**   **Matthew 4:17**

If we look closely at the word repent, we learn that our modern use does not match the Biblical definition. In today's vernacular, repentance refers to feelings or emotions of sincere regret and remorse about one's wrongdoing or sin. But the original Greek word, *metanoia*, is much more than emotions and regret. *Metanoia* is used 22 times in the New Testament and means to change one's mind or purpose with action. The repentance Jesus was preaching wasn't defined by feelings but by a change of attitude and action concerning one's sin.

The Gospel of Luke gives us insight into Matthew's own call to be a disciple. Matthew was sitting in a tax booth, engaged in one of the most despised professions for anyone in Israel, a tax collector. When Jesus came by and said, "Follow me," Matthew left everything behind to follow Him; he immediately changed his course (repented).

Then, Luke tells us that Matthew held a banquet for tax collectors and sinners. The Pharisees were not impressed and complained to the disciples, "Why do you eat and drink with tax collectors and sinners?"

Listen to Jesus's response to their criticism: "It is not the healthy who need a doctor, but the sick." Then he says, "I've not come to call the righteous, but sinners to repentance." While the self-righteous Pharisees saw sinful people as rebellious lawbreakers who should be tossed into jail, Jesus saw sinners as sick people who needed to be made well. Jesus knew that true spiritual wellness begins with repentance.

Later in Luke's Gospel, we gain another insight into repentance. During Jesus's day, there was an incident in which a group of Galileans were traveling south to Jerusalem to worship the Lord at the temple there. The Romans slaughtered them, and in an awful act of brute power, Pilate, who would later condemn Jesus to the cross, took the blood of those Galileans, mixed the blood in the poured offering, and forced the Jewish priests to pour that on the altar.

When told about this atrocity, Jesus answered, "Do you think that these Galileans were worse sinners than all the other Galileans because they suffered in this way? I tell you, no! But unless you repent, you too will all perish" (Luke 13:2-3).

Wow! Is this a new troubling side of Jesus you didn't know about and weren't expecting? Too judgmental for your liking?

Jesus was serious about repentance because He knew Hell and God's judgment were real. And He also knew that the only rescue is true repentance.

The Jewish people Jesus was speaking to understood that God was both rich in mercy and stern in justice. He was a rewarder for those who followed after righteousness and a strict judge of the rebellious and sinfully arrogant.

Are you familiar with the story of Jonah? The Israelites knew it well. Jonah was called to preach repentance to the wicked people of Nineveh. Instead of going to those evil people, Jonah tried to run away. But after a storm, being swallowed by a fish, and being vomited out on the shore of Nineveh, Jonah started to preach of coming calamity unless the people repented. Surprisingly, the king of Nineveh and the people turned to God.

The king gave this proclamation: "By the decree of the king and his nobles: Do not let people or animals, herds or flocks, taste anything; do not let them eat or drink. But let people and animals be covered with sackcloth. Let everyone call urgently on God. Let them give up their evil ways and their violence. Who knows? God may yet relent and with compassion turn from his fierce anger so that we will not perish" (Jonah 3:6).

If there was ever a story from the Bible illustrating what true repentance looks like, it's this. The Ninevites did not scream and cry and throw dust on their heads; they changed their ways, and God relented. The city was spared from the impending destruction.

Jesus used this story of the Ninevites to challenge the Jewish people. "The men of Nineveh will stand up at the judgment with this generation and condemn it; for they repented at the preaching of Jonah, and now something greater than Jonah is here" (Matthew 12:41). Jesus was reminding His listeners that the Ninevites weren't the chosen people; they were a pagan culture that God had mercy on. And when those people are called to the witness stand, they will condemn God's chosen people for not repenting when not the prophet Jonah but the Son of God Himself was preaching to them.

One of my (Todd's) favorite Bible stories is when Jesus heals a crippled man at the Pool of Bethesda. The man had been crippled all 38 years of his life. For 38 years, he was begging in that same place, lying on a mat, soiled and stinking and rotting, and Jesus healed him.

Even though he'd been healed, we find he continued sinning. Look at this verse: "Later Jesus found him at the temple and said to him, 'See, you are well again. Stop sinning, or something worse may happen to you'" (John 5:14).

That needs to be underlined in your Bible. It is the same thing Jesus is saying to our world today, to some of us—stop sinning, or something worse may happen to you. You and I can be sorry about our sins all day or even all of our lives and never repent. We can wallow in shame, be perpetually sad, and cry over our sins; but Jesus demands we turn away from sin and change our ways to follow Him. A true disciple of Jesus lives a life marked by repentance.

In a familiar parable, Jesus told the story of a lost sheep. A shepherd had a hundred sheep, and one wandered off from the flock, got lost and trapped in some barren place, and the shepherd went after it to rescue it. When he found it, he brought it back to the flock and then rejoiced to all his neighbors— what was lost was now found. Jesus explains the meaning behind this parable: "I tell you in the same way there will be more rejoicing in Heaven over one sinner who repents than over ninety-nine righteous persons who do not need to repent" (Luke 15:7).

Without Jesus we are lost sheep, lost people, sick people in need of a doctor. Let's be reminded that God so loved us that He sent our

Shepherd, our Savior, to find us, rescue us, and heal us. When we repent of our sins and become a follower of Jesus, the angels in Heaven rejoice!

Read: 2 Corinthians 7:10, Revelation 3:19, John 3:17

Reflect: When was a time when you were sorry for your sin, but you didn't repent?

Pray: God, help me to follow You completely. If there are any areas I am holding on to sin and need to repent, please make those clear.

CHAPTER 5

Take Up Your Cross

We need men of the cross with the message of the cross, bearing the marks of the cross.   *—Vance Hevener*

In his book *Kingdoms in Conflict*, Chuck Colson gives an account of Poland in 1984 when Prime Minister Jaruzelski ordered all crucifixes to be removed from all public institutions including schools. The Catholic bishops stood against this ban, which was stirring up anger and resentment throughout the country. Colson writes:

> One zealous, communist school administrator in Poland had seven large crucifixes removed from lecture halls where they had hung since the school's founding in the 20s. Days later a group of parents entered the school and hung more crosses, the administrator promptly had them taken down as well. The next day two thirds of the school's 600 students staged a sit in. When heavily armed riot police arrived, the students were forced into the streets, then they marched with crucifixes held high to a nearby church where they were joined by 2500 other students from nearby schools for a morning of prayer in support of the protest. Soldiers surrounded the church but the photographs from inside of students holding their crosses high above their heads flashed around the world. So did the words of the priest who delivered the message to that weeping congregation that morning. He said, "There is no Poland without the cross."[3]

Now, decades later, I (Todd) wonder if the Polish people still feel that way. Would there still be such an outrage against the removal of the crucifix? And what about America, a nation forged out of Christian belief and the Bible? Would Americans today say there is no America without the cross? And what about the church? Do we believe there is no church without the cross?

The truth is, there's no true Christianity, no true discipleship, without the cross. I'm not just talking about the idea of the cross. I'm not pointing to a crucifix hanging in our church. I'm talking about not just understanding the doctrine of the cross but living by it, taking up our cross, and losing our lives, if necessary, in the pursuit of Christ. That is precisely what Jesus calls us to do. It's the definition of a follower of Jesus.

> **"Then Jesus said to his disciples, 'Whoever wants to be my disciple must deny themselves and take up their cross and follow me. For whoever wants to save their life will lose it, but whoever loses their life for me will find it.'"**
> **Matthew 16:24-25**

Luke and Mark echo these words from Matthew. Luke adds that taking up our cross is a daily activity, and Mark adds, "For whoever wants to save their life will lose it, but whoever loses their life for me and for the gospel will save it. What good is it for someone to gain the whole world, yet forfeit their soul?'" (Mark 8:35-36).

There are many good, holy, and fruitful things Christians are called to do. We are to model Jesus's kindness, purity, prayerfulness, and service to others. But in His own words, there is no following Him without the cross.

The disciples must have shuddered when they heard these words because they were living in the days of real crosses. The Roman cross was one of the most wicked inventions of man, a diabolical, awful way to take a life. The disciples had seen capital punishment meted out to criminals on the cross. They'd heard the shrieks and the cries of dying men struggling just to breathe. Now Jesus is saying the most alarming thing, that His true followers must accompany Him to crucifixion!

It might help to get a historical picture of what bearing a cross looked like. While we have seen images of Jesus carrying a full cross, more accurately, a condemned man would carry just the cross piece. This piece was heavy. Remember how, in the Gospels, we learn that Jesus fell under the weight and someone else had to come and carry His cross? After carrying the cross through the streets with people jeering, the condemned criminal would arrive at the crucifixion sight. They would be stripped of all of their clothes, laid down, their hands stretched against that cross piece, and there would be nails driven into those hands. Then they would be hoisted up in inexpressible agony, with their feet crossed and another nail driven through.

In addition to the physical pain, the cross marked you as a wicked criminal. It signified shame and condemnation. Centuries before Jesus hung on a cross, Isaiah wrote, "He was assigned a grave with the wicked, and with the rich in his death" (Isaiah 53:9). When Jesus calls His followers to take up their crosses, He indicates they will be marked. Throughout history, to be a Christian often meant to be hated and despised.

When Jesus told the twelve disciples about the brutal death He would experience, Thomas (yes, the one we know as Doubting Thomas) said one of the bravest things any of the disciples had ever said: "Then Thomas (also known as Didymus) said to the rest of the disciples, 'Let us also go, that we may die with him'" (John 11:16).

Thomas was saying, "Let's get in line and follow Him to the cross." Today, I want to ask myself and I want you to ask yourself, am I doing that? Am I living that Christ-life? Not just church attendance, not just doing good, or just being faithful in ministry and service, but being determined to take up the cross and even experience martyrdom and death.

Elizabeth Elliot wrote a book outlining the story of her husband Jim Elliot and four other missionaries, who went to Ecuador in the 1950s to share the Gospel. My copy of *Gates of Splendor* is well-worn and dog-eared from much reading. Elliot tells how these five men established a church and baptized many converts to Christ, then hungered to go deeper into the jungle to the Ecuadorian Indians living in primitive conditions with no contact with civilization. After devising a plan and carefully working it through, the men journeyed into the jungle to make the first contact with these Indians. Tragically, those missionaries lost their lives—speared to death—by those they had hoped to bring to Christ.

Elizabeth's writing shares her husband's perspective on life and ministry. One well-known quote from Jim's journal is, "He's no fool who gives up that which he cannot keep, to gain that which he cannot lose."[4] Jim Elliot understood discipleship and cross-bearing.

It would be rare for most of us to be speared to death in an Ecuadorian jungle. Chances are good that most of us will never be crucified, put to death, or even tortured for following Jesus. But the call is still the same. In a thousand ways, big and small, we deny ourselves and crucify our flesh every day. In Galatians 5:24, we are told, "Those who belong to Christ Jesus have crucified the flesh with its passions and desires." I'm ashamed to say that many of us who have been Christians for years haven't fully put to death the lust and the passions and the desires of life. Let alone lie down and die for the Lord. We have not embraced true discipleship.

Listen to Matthew again: "For whoever wants to save their life will lose it, but whoever loses their life for me will find it" (Matthew 16:24-25). Being a disciple demands absolute allegiance. Whatever path is marked out for us, we have the same call: To take up our cross, let go of our own life, and follow Jesus.

Read: Mark 10:32-34, Philippians 2:5-8, Hebrews 12:1-3

Reflect: What does it mean for me to take up the cross of Jesus today, right now?

Pray: Jesus, You sacrificed Your life for me, taking on excruciating pain and shame. Help me to learn from Your example and give up my life for You. Show me any areas I am holding back from Your command to take up the cross and to die daily.

CHAPTER 6

LOVE ME

Jesus cannot be just liked. His claims make us either kill him or crown him.
—*Timothy Keller*

Do you like Jesus? Admire Him?

Or do you truly love Him?

One of Jesus's simplest yet most challenging commands is His command to "love Me." Jesus doesn't suggest that we love Him; He demands it. And He tells us that it is the greatest of all the commands. Love is the defining mark of a disciple of Jesus.

> **"'Teacher, which is the greatest commandment in the Law?' Jesus replied: 'Love the Lord your God with all your heart and with all your soul and with all your mind. This is the first and greatest commandment.'"** Matthew 22:36-38

The type of love Jesus is talking about is much deeper than like or admiration. It is all-consuming. He is saying, *you must love me absolutely. You must love me most, you must love me best, and there is no one you should love more than me.*

In Matthew 10:37, Jesus goes as far as to say, "Anyone who loves their father or mother more than me is not worthy of me; anyone who loves their son or daughter more than me is not worthy of me."

How do you feel when you hear those words? Does it feel demanding, even egotistical? To me (Todd), these words can sound like those of a crazed, possessive, obsessive lover. What may make this so difficult for us to process is that when we compare our love for our family to our love for Jesus, our love for Jesus may not even come close by comparison.

We must understand that Jesus is not saying we shouldn't love our father, mother, or children. In chapter one, we already looked at how Jesus commanded us to love others sacrificially. But our love for others must always come second to our love for Jesus.

I think that may be what's wrong with the church today. We like Jesus, we admire Him, we respect and honor Him, and we pray to Him. But we don't love Him greatly. We don't love Him most.

I don't know about you, but it just doesn't come naturally to me to love the Lord this much. While I do love Jesus and my Heavenly Father, I need to love them more. In studying this command, I searched the Scripture for help. I want to share with you a few key ways I uncovered that can help us learn to love God more.

KEY #1 - KNOW HIM MORE

In Ephesians, the Apostle Paul prayed for the church in Ephesus to know God better (Ephesians 1:17) through the revelation of the Holy Spirit and that they would "grasp how wide and long and high and deep is the love of Christ, and to know this love that surpasses knowledge" (Ephesians 3:19).

Is it possible that you love God very little because you don't know Him very well?

No one wants you to know Jesus more than the Holy Spirit. No one wants to assist you, to enable you to do that supernaturally more than the Holy Spirit. Learning from Paul's prayer, we can ask the Holy Spirit to help us know Jesus better and to love Him even more.

KEY #2 - REMAIN IN HIM

Calvin Miller wrote, "A passion to obey Christ is born out of our relationship with him. The more we love him, the more we want him to be a part of our affairs."[5] In order to love God more, we need to be connected to Him, involving Him in every aspect of our lives.

In John 15, Jesus instructs His disciples to remain in Him so they can be fruitful, just as a branch must remain in the vine to bear fruit. He goes even further to say that when we keep His commands, we will remain in His love just as He kept His Father's commands and remained in His love (John 15:10). As we stay attached to the vine, as we remain in Him, and as we keep His commands, the love of God is expressed in us and through us. Jesus's love completes us. Or said differently, we are incomplete without His love.

KEY #3 - NOT LOVING THE WORLD

In I John 2:15-16, we learn that loving the world and loving God are in direct competition with each other. The Apostle John writes, "Do not love the world or anything in the world. If anyone loves the world, love for the Father is not in them. For everything in the world, the lust of the flesh, the lust of the eyes, and the pride of life, comes not from the Father but from the world."

These verses are often misunderstood to mean that if you love the world, God will quit loving you. But that is not what is being communicated. Instead of God's love being reduced, we see that when we love the world, it takes up space and displaces our love for the Father. Maybe we are having a hard time loving God because our hearts are full of love, lust, and desire for the world. Do you love movies, books, carnality, sexual immorality, and wrong relationships? Do you have an appetite for worldly pleasure and wonder why you don't love Jesus more?

KEY #4 - LOVING OTHERS

In Ephesians 4:16, we are given a picture of the body of Christ "joined and held together by every supporting ligament, grows and builds itself up in love, as each part does its work." We are all called to be full-grown fruit-bearing disciples of Christ. Part of that call is intentionally discovering your spiritual gift and putting it into practice in the church and in the community.

When we serve others with the love of Christ through the power of the Holy Spirit, the love of Christ changes the world and changes us. Are you living a life committed to loving and serving others? As each part of Christ's body does its work, it is love in bloom, growing more vital and passionate every day.

KEY #5 - BEING LIKE HIM

In 1 John 4:16-17 John writes, "God is love, whoever lives in love lives in God and God in them. This is how love is made complete among us so that we will have confidence on the day of judgment: In this world we are like Jesus." We are called to nothing less than to live like Jesus. Maybe our lack of love for God is because we're not living like Him, and we just want to do what we want to do.

When I was a young college student, I heard a speaker named Tommy Oaks tell a story I've never forgotten. On a snowy Saturday evening, while he was preparing his sermon for the next day, Tommy received a late-night call for help. A woman in the church was married to the town drunk, and the man hadn't come home. This wasn't the first time Tommy had been asked to go searching for her husband. Despite Tommy's wife warning him of the weather danger, he headed out to help. At first, Tommy was annoyed, but he felt Jesus say, "Tommy, this isn't how to do this, this isn't right, this is not what I've called you to. Think about how you're feeling. Tonight, try doing this the way I would."

At that moment, Tommy became excited about the challenge, thinking about what the night might be like if he were Jesus. He imagined the thorns on Jesus's head and the nail holes in His hands. He felt the pain in Jesus's side from the sword and began to weep as he drove through the familiar streets of his town.

When he arrived at the woman's house, instead of annoyance, Tommy saw her for the first time through Jesus's eyes. He then searched for hours on that cold night until he found the man passed out on the floor of a supply room in the back of a bar. Tommy got down on his knees weeping, then struggled to get the man home, feeling the pain of Jesus in his hands and feet. After helping the man's wife get him into bed, Tommy finally returned home. He told us that never in his life had he been more prepared to preach on a Sunday morning.

We are called to live like Jesus. When we are more like Jesus, we experience His love and learn to love Him even more.

Read: John 14:15, 1 John 2:5, 1 John 4:12, Ephesians 1:17-19

Reflect: Do you truly love God?

Pray: God, I want to love You above all else. Holy Spirit, teach me to love You with all my heart, soul, mind and strength.

CHAPTER 7

WORSHIP THE FATHER

In worship, God captures your heart; when he's got it, then the real work begins.
—*Matt Redman*

In early 2023, I (Stacey) had the honor of traveling with my wife Sherri to Robin's Nest Children's Home high in the mountains of Jamaica. Only months before our dear friends, Chris and Cheran Hewitt, had answered the call of Christ, sold everything they had, packed up their two small children, and moved to serve as directors at the remote children's home.

Robin's Nest is perched at the very top of a mountain, and from many of the buildings, the ground falls away sharply into the valley floor below. The views from our bunk room revealed miles of jungle, with views stretching clear to the ocean in Montego Bay.

While I have many great memories from serving through the week, there is one memory in particular that stands above the rest. One evening as I stood and watched from a distance, a group of little children gathered together with their leaders and started to sing. They had no mics, no fancy background track, or instruments, they didn't have anything but their heart and their voices; they just sang to God. Their worship was powerful. The sounds of their voices carried through the open-air windows and out into the jungle-filled valleys below. I'm not sure I have experienced worship that was any purer and more acceptable to God.

Maybe you've had a similar experience.

True worship moves people and moves our hearts, yet there's something mysterious and hard to define about it. The command of Jesus we are looking at today will focus on that very thing.

> **"The time is coming, indeed it's here now, when true worshipers will worship the Father in spirit and in truth. The Father is looking for those who will worship him that way."**
> **John 4:23**

When Jesus spoke these words, there was a disagreement in the culture about where true worship should be shared, how it should be shared, and who should share it. The Jewish people living in Jerusalem believed that true worship could only happen in the temple of God located in Jerusalem. Some miles away, another group called the Samaritans believed that true worship could only occur on a particular mountain.

The Jewish people looked at the Samaritans as secondary citizens, half-breeds that had broken God's command, because they had wandered away from Judaism and married into the local pagan community. The rift between these people was so strong that they refused to even be in each other's presence. They would walk many miles around to avoid each other's territory.

But Jesus, in His bold and uncompromising way, saw no boundaries; He only saw people. He walked straight into the dusty and dry Samaritan village of Sychar one day. Thirsty from the travel, Jesus sat down at the well and found a woman. He asked her for a drink and began to converse with her. In only a few minutes, Jesus started to unravel her life, sharing things about her that she had definitely never told Him and quite possibly, anyone else. This Samaritan woman quickly realized she was not speaking to an ordinary Jewish man.

In John 4:19-20, we hear her processing this encounter, "'Sir,' the woman said, 'you must be a prophet. So tell me, why is it that you Jews insist that Jerusalem is the only place of worship, while we Samaritans claim it is here at Mount Gerizim, where our ancestors worshiped?'"

Jesus cuts to the chase, refusing to enter into the generations-old argument of who is worshiping where and how, and instead declares that true worshippers worship God in spirit and in truth. And God is paying attention, looking for these true worshipers.

If there is true worship, logic tells us there is also artificial worship. Matthew 15:8-9 points to this counterfeit worship: "These people honor me with their lips, but their hearts are far from me. They worship me in vain." God is telling us it is possible to come to church and go through all of the actions, stand up at the right time, sing all of the right words in perfect pitch and key at the right time, and still miss the mark.

I wonder if our worship meets the criterion, the standard that God is looking for in our worship. The Greek word for worshipers that Jesus used here can be defined as *adore, adoration, and deep love.*[6] What comes to mind when you think of adoration?

I think of this past year when I had the opportunity to walk my daughter down the aisle. It was an amazing, emotional experience. I'll never forget as I held her on my arm, and we walked out the door and rounded a corner, and her new husband saw her for the very first time. The adoration of pure love and appreciation that they felt so deeply for each other was evident.

I also remember when our children were very small, and they would get up in the middle of the night, multiple times throughout the night. Their cry wakes you up; you walk into their room, pick them up, and rock them, trying desperately to get them back to sleep. Then comes that moment when they fall asleep—you stare down at this beautiful, perfect, sweet, smoothed-skin baby God has given you. You feel that overwhelming adoration, deep love, and affection.

When Jesus referred to worshipers, He had one kind of person, one kind of attitude in mind: someone who loves and adores God above all else. When you worship, is that what you feel toward God? Like a husband seeing his bride for the first time or a parent lovingly looking at their child?

We need to define one more key term in Jesus's command in this short Scripture: the word "worship" itself. What is the act of worship that is true? What is it that true worshipers do?

You may have noticed that everyone has their own style of worship. On any given Sunday, if you look around most churches, you see all kinds of approaches to worship. Some people just have an arms-folded, lips-sealed approach. They are there and focused intently on the words; if they sing, it would take their focus away. There's another type that moves beyond the stand and the stare. They have a little sway, staying in time with the music. Another type is getting a full aerobic workout; they have all their steps in before they leave the service. God loves it all!

The Greek word for worship that Jesus uses might surprise you. The Greek word *proskuneo* that He uses means t*o bow down, to prostrate oneself before another, to show deep reverence and submission.*[7] Worship is the act of submitting ourselves in deep homage and humility before God.

I don't believe that this means that the only true worship will be carried out on our knees or lying on our faces, but I do wonder if you can fully arrive at true worship if you are not practicing that at some point in your personal devotional life. All I can say for sure is that for Jesus Christ, true worship begins with a heart bowed down in humility before an Almighty God. When these two realities come together, a heart of genuine love and adoration for God mixed with an attitude of humility and prostration before Him, then we are nearing true worship—the kind that God deserves and even commands.

Is it any wonder when we come into church having ignored our relationship with Jesus all week that we struggle to worship Him? In John 3:6 Jesus explains, "Flesh gives birth to flesh, but the Spirit gives birth to spirit." When our flesh leads the way, it results in a self-centered, self-promoting heart that refuses to bend its knee in humility to anything other than itself.

On the other hand, when we are guided by the Spirit of Christ who lives in us, He reforms our desires and our actions. We are driven by our realization of our need for Christ and His great and undeserved grace, forgiveness, and love. That spirit-filled, selfless heart blesses God and praises God. And we worship with a heart filled with humble thanksgiving and praise.

Read: Matthew 16:17, Matthew 22:37, John 16:13, Romans 8:14-15

Reflect: Is my worship true and genuine, full of adoration for God?

Pray: God, You are worthy of worship. I humbly come before You and confess that I need You. I declare Your goodness and surrender myself to Your will.

SECTION 2

INTIMACY WITH THE FATHER

Now this is eternal life: that they know you, the only true God, and Jesus Christ, whom you have sent.

John 17:3

CHAPTER 8

COME TO ME

The command of Jesus is hard, unutterably hard, for those who try to resist it. But for those who willingly submit, the yoke is easy, and the burden is light. —Dietrich Bonhoeffer

Have you ever experienced a "come to Jesus" moment?

In popular culture, a "come to Jesus" moment might be a crisis, a confrontation, or a near-death experience. Miriam-Webster's dictionary defines it this way: "Outside of religious context, come to Jesus refers to a meeting or a moment where one undergoes a difficult but positive and powerful realization or change in character or behavior."[8]

The invitation to come to God distinguishes Christianity from all other world religions. Even outside of a spiritual context, it is understood that to come to Jesus means to change, to leave something behind, and to move in a new direction. When Jesus came to His own people, Israel, they were weighed down by a religious order that demanded sacrifice, absolute obedience, no wiggle room, no grace, and no mercy; it was a heavy yoke around their necks and a great burden to carry.

Listen carefully to His words to the weary and burdened who've carried around a load of guilt and shame, never feeling good enough for God. Tenderly, the Savior says, "Come to me, be unburdened, cast off the demands and restraint of that old religion, and find me, find rest and life eternal." Jesus doesn't call us to religious practices; He calls us to come to Him.

> **"Then Jesus said, 'Come to me, all of you who are weary and carry heavy burdens, and I will give you rest. Take my yoke upon you. Let me teach you, because I am humble and gentle at heart, and you will find rest for your souls. For my yoke is easy to bear, and the burden I give you is light.'"**
> **Matthew 11:28-30**

While we see that coming to Jesus provides a release and great unburdening, we also see that Jesus doesn't promise that we will be free from burdens. Rather, His words imply we *will have* burdens. Using Jesus's own teaching, I (Todd) want to identify two burdens that accompany those who follow Him because before we can understand the rest, we need to understand the burdens we carry.

The first burden is this: Yours will be an isolated journey.

Do you remember when Jesus told the parable of two roads? There's a broad road that many find. It is a road teaming with people that ends in death. And there's another road with a very narrow gate. Listen to how Jesus describes it in Matthew chapter 7:14: "But the gateway to life is very narrow, and the road is difficult, and only a few ever find it."

In a world hurling toward destruction down a broad path, true believers experience increasing isolation. The world offers the best movies, the best music, all kinds of promises, made by a thousand seductive voices. That's where we were when Jesus called us. Some of us are still struggling to swim against that current and stay on task to enter through the narrow gate and walk on the narrow path. But Jesus is calling, "Come to me. Stay on course; choose this path."

The second burden is this: Those on the broad path will eventually hate us.

Jesus predicted this in Luke 21:16-17: "Even those closest to you—your parents, brothers, relatives, and friends—will betray you. They will even kill some of you. And everyone will hate you because you are my followers." This prediction made two thousand years ago is still true today.

Recently, I read an excerpt by Mary Eberstadt titled "Religious Freedom and Its Enemies." Listen to this description of America:

> This new vigorous, secularism has catapulted mockery of Christianity and other forms of religious traditionalism into the mainstream and set a new low for what counts as critical

criticism of people's most cherished beliefs. In some pretext the "Faith of our Fathers" is more controversial than ever before. Some of the faithful have paid unexpected prices for their beliefs lately. A teacher in New Jersey suspended for giving a student a Bible. The football coach in Washington was placed on leave for saying a prayer on the field at the end of the game. The fire chief in Atlanta fired for self-publishing a book defending Christian moral teaching. The marine was court-martialed for pasting a Bible verse above her desk and other examples of the new intolerance, anti-Christian activist hurling smears like, bigot and hater and racist at Americans who hold long held traditional beliefs about marriage and the unborn. Activists have targeted homeschooling now, for being a Christian thing. Atheist Richard Dawkins and others have even called homeschooling tantamount to child abuse. Student groups like Intervarsity have been kicked off campuses, Christian charities, adoption agencies, hospitals, crisis pregnancy centers have all become objects of attack.[9]

Answering the call to come to Jesus will cost you. Burdens will accompany your decision. You will be disliked, even despised. But let's be clear: Jesus isn't the burden. Jesus carries our burdens and lightens them.

In John 7, Jesus and His disciples are in Jerusalem celebrating the weeklong festival of the Feast of Tabernacles. Here, Jesus stands up in the crowd and shouts, "Anyone who is thirsty may come to me!" (John 7:37). Jesus offers to quench our thirsty souls. In John 6:35, Jesus describes Himself as the bread of life: "I am the bread of life. Whoever comes to me will never be hungry again." Jesus can satisfy our deepest hunger and desires.

But despite Jesus's offer of rest for our souls, a drink that will never leave us thirsty again, and the bread of life from Heaven itself, few people respond to Jesus's invitation to "come."

Do you ever wonder why people refuse to come to Jesus? It's a very simple answer from Jesus Himself. Mark this down. "And the judgment is based on this fact: God's light came into the world, but people loved the darkness more than the light, for their actions were evil. All who do evil hate the light and refuse to go near it for fear their sins will be exposed" (John 3:19-20).

Many, many people just love darkness. They want to be on a dark path that leads to destruction because they love it there. They've grown used to that black hole. God sent His one and only Son into a dark, dying world with this message: "Come to me—come to me all who are weary, burdened, and heavy-laden, and I will give you rest." But Jesus also made another statement in John 14:6, "I am the way, the truth, and the life. No one can come to the Father except through me."

Jesus's call to come is exclusive. His is not one path of many. He made a singular way through His body on the cross. When we follow Jesus, people will consider us arrogant and pompous for believing He is the only way to God. But Jesus bids us to come. Yes, it will be isolating, and we'll be hated. But Jesus will carry our burdens. When we draw close to Him, we will experience great joy and unspeakable hope. We have the promise of heaven, the love of our Heavenly Father, strength from the Holy Spirit to endure, and true rest for our souls.

Read: John 4:7-14, John 5:39-40, Matthew 23:37, Revelation 22:17

Reflect: What burdens are you carrying as a result of following Jesus? Have you come to Him with those burdens?

Pray: Jesus, following You is demanding. It is not always easy, but it is always worth it. Thank You for inviting me to come. Thank You for bearing my burdens and walking down the narrow path with me.

CHAPTER 9

REMAIN IN ME

> *There are not two Christs—an easy-going one for easy-going Christians, and a suffering, toiling one for exceptional believers. There is only one Christ. Are you willing to abide in Him, and thus to bear much fruit?* —Geraldine Taylor, Missionary to China

Throughout Jesus's teachings and the New Testament writing, we repeatedly see references to bearing fruit. For example, listen to this pastoral prayer Paul prayed for the church in Colossae: "We continually ask God to fill you with the knowledge of his will through all the wisdom and understanding that the Spirit gives, so that you may live a life worthy of the Lord and please him in every way, bearing fruit in every good work, growing in the knowledge of God" (Colossians 1:9-10).

Imagine with me (Todd) what that prayer would look like if it were answered in us, the church. What would it look like if we all were pleasing to God, bearing fruit in every kind of ministry and good work, growing together in the knowledge of God, so Spirit-filled, so knowledgeable of God? Fruitful people.

We are going to look at the simple secret to bearing fruit. This basic equation for bearing fruit might surprise you. Bearing good fruit doesn't demand a lot from us; it only requires obedience. Real fruit comes from the work of the Holy Spirit in us. Jesus bears fruit through us.

We also should be soberly reminded that we have been saved to bear fruit. It is a command, not an option. Fruitlessness in our lives is evidence that we have pulled away from Jesus. It is evidence that we are detaching ourselves from the source of fruit, backing up, backing away, and headed to danger.

In Luke 13, Jesus tells a troubling story that illustrates this truth. A man had a fig tree in his vineyard. For three years, he looked at it, expecting it to bear fruit, but there was none. Frustrated, he demanded the tree be cut down, no longer taking up valuable soil in his vineyard. But the servant tending the garden pleaded for one more year. He promised to dig around the fig tree and fertilize it. Then, after one year, if it didn't bear fruit, he would cut it down.

And that's where the parable ends. We don't know what happens to the tree. Did the servant's care make a difference? Or was the tree cut down due to uselessness? Those questions are left unanswered, but the story calls us to examine our own lives.

Jesus is using this story to teach us about our fruitfulness or lack thereof. I believe He is the master of the vineyard, and the servant is the Holy Spirit. Like the fig tree, we have an opportunity through the work of the Holy Spirit to bear fruit, or we fail to yield fruit because of our disobedience and rebellion to the Holy Spirit.

In Jerusalem, days before His death, the atmosphere was heavy as Jesus shared a meal with His disciples in an upper room. While only Jesus understood the cross looming before Him, they all knew something bad was coming. After Jesus washed their feet and they shared the cup of communion, they walked toward the Garden of Gethsemane, where Jesus would spend the night praying in agony.

Along the way, Jesus stopped for one last important lesson, the last chapter of His teachings. Part of this discourse is found in John 15. Jesus gave an illustration, and seven times He commanded His followers to bear fruit and eleven times to remain in Him. The word "remain" is a relational term conveying Jesus's heart: *Please continue to be present in my company, please don't break our fellowship, please don't leave, please don't depart, remain.*

> **"Remain in me, as I also remain in you. No branch can bear fruit by itself; it must remain in the vine. Neither can you bear fruit unless you remain in me. I am the vine; you are the branches."** John 15:4-5a

Like the parable of the fig tree, this is an object lesson the disciples clearly understood. These men had been in vineyards, probably even labored in vineyards. They understood that the source that fed the grapes was the root. The vine drew its sustenance from the earth's nutrients, producing leaves that gathered the sun and sped on nutrients to the end of the branch until fruit appeared. In the same way, Jesus is our source of life, light, and fruit.

Jesus continued, "If you remain in me and I in you, you will bear much fruit; apart from me you can do nothing. If you do not remain in me, you are like a branch that is thrown away and withers; such branches are picked up, thrown into the fire and burned" (John 15:5b-6).

Whether you remain or don't remain, there are determined outcomes. The branch that remains is promised fruitfulness, but like the fruitless tree in Luke, Jesus paints the picture of fiery judgment and condemnation for the disobedient and the rebellious.

I want to stop and acknowledge this is challenging theology for many of us. First, we are challenged by the fact that despite all of His mercy, God sternly requires us to bear fruit. We also find it challenging because we might have been taught to see this passage about branches being cut off as talking about non-believers. But in John 15, Jesus isn't speaking to large crowds of unsaved people. He is speaking intimately with His disciples, those who follow Him.

John 16:1 gives us an important context for this teaching: "All this I have told you so that you will not fall away." Jesus knew that very evening, the disciples would all abandon Him. He prayed for them to be restored, to be strong, to come back, and to go out and change the world. Like these disciples, we have the same capacity in us to fall away. Sometimes, we move away because of sin. Other times, it is fear, laziness, seduction, or even boredom.

Jesus is warning us: When we are that tree that is not going to bear fruit, that is just taking up space, He will cut us down and replace us with something or someone that will bear fruit. Bearing fruit is not open for discussion; it is not an option—it is a requirement.

Remaining in Christ is much more than consistent church attendance. It is participating in something divine. God is working in me and through me. In II Peter 1, the Apostle Peter explains the spiritual nature of bearing fruit:

> His divine power has given us everything we need for a godly life through our knowledge of him who has called by his own glory and goodness, through these he has given us his very great and precious promises so that through them you may participate in the divine nature. For this very reason, make every effort to add to your faith goodness, to goodness knowledge, to knowledge

self-control, to self-control perseverance, to perseverance godliness, to godliness mutual affection, to mutual affection love. For if you possess these qualities in increasing measure, they will keep you from being ineffective and unproductive in your knowledge of our Lord Jesus Christ. But whoever does not have them is nearsighted, blind, forgetting that they have been cleansed from their past sins. (II Peter 1:3-9)

God's Spirit is at work in us, providing us with everything we need; all the nutrients, and all the tools we need to bear fruit. More than that, if we are willing vessels, we are participating in the divine nature. As we open ourselves up through this connectivity, we are filled, and we produce, and we pass on in our lives light and hope and blessing and peace and promise.

Read: John 15:1-16, Romans 11:17-24, Philippians 1:9-11

Reflect: Is your life bearing fruit, showing the evidence of remaining in Jesus? Are you increasing in godliness and effectiveness? Or are you unproductive and ineffective, resulting from falling away from Jesus?

Pray: God, help me to remain in You. I want my life to be fruitful for Your purpose. Fill me with the fullness of Your Spirit and make me effective for Your Kingdom.

CHAPTER 10

HEAR MY WORDS

The willingness to obey every word from God is critical to hearing God speak. —Henry T. Blackaby

Are you a good listener? When someone else is talking, are you thinking about what you are going to say when they shut up, or are you actively listening? Keeping that answer in mind—what would your spouse or your co-workers have to say on this subject?

By definition, active listening is "a communication skill that involves going beyond simply hearing words that another person speaks but also seeking to understand the meaning and intent behind them. It requires being an active participant in the communication process."[10]

Larry King, a great TV personality who interviewed over a thousand people, said, "I remind myself every morning: Nothing I say this day will teach me anything. So, if I'm going to learn, I must do it by listening."[11]

Sadly, I (Todd) have developed the poor art of inactive listening. It happens most frequently when my sweet wife Karen is talking to me. After a long day of actively listening to many people—I clock out. Then when Karen tries to explain something to me, I've trained myself to have an intent look and nod occasionally, but she sees the glaze in my eyes and knows I'm not there.

Over and over, in various ways, Jesus instructed His followers, *listen to me, actively listen to me.* I love this Scripture from Luke's Gospel:

"He who has ears to hear, let him hear!" Luke 8:8

In today's vernacular, we might say it this way, "Do you have ears? Put them on because I've got something very important to tell you." It reminds me of a first-grade teacher prompting her unruly students, "Eyes, eyes," or "ears, ears!" Jesus is asking us - *do you have ears?* Let's put on our ears today and listen carefully to what Jesus has to say as He delivers to us the commands of God.

Go with me in your imagination back to Israel in the time of Jesus. Put yourself in the community; the word is out, Jesus the Rabbi is coming to speak, and you rush out with everybody else. You want to see who this guy is and what He has to say. Maybe you want to see Him perform a miracle. You gather with the crowd, and Jesus stands up to speak. You see a young, recently out-of-work carpenter who has come literally out of nowhere. His appearance is nondescript. But His words pull you in.

Wouldn't it be amazing if we had a recording of His teaching— to hear His voice, to know what He sounded like, see what His delivery looked like, His gestures, His back and forth with the crowd?

When Jesus was speaking, He was speaking God's words. Listening to Jesus equates to listening to His Father. Hebrews 1:1-2 explains it this way: "In the past God spoke to our ancestors through the prophets at many times and in various ways, but in these last days he has spoken to us by his Son, whom he appointed heir of all things, and through whom also he made the universe."

We have the words of God spoken through Jesus and recorded in the New Testament in the Gospels. Jesus is speaking to us in these last days. And if the last days were happening when Jesus was on earth, how much closer to the end are we now? We should be tuned in and paying attention because the days are short.

Unfortunately, many people have reduced the teaching of Jesus to something that doesn't even resemble the New Testament. They make His words more comfortable, saying He just came to tell us all to get along, that everything will be alright, and to just love each other.

But when we read the Gospels, we see that Jesus was direct and often controversial. Consider His statement in Luke 5:32: "I came to call sinners to repentance." What would you have thought if you were in the crowd hearing a declaration like that? We know that the religious leaders of Jesus's day were often offended, even accusing Him of high blasphemy and religious treason.

Here is another example: "Very truly I tell you, whoever hears my word and believes him who sent me has eternal life and will not be judged but has crossed over from death to life. Very truly I tell you, a time is coming and has now come when the dead will hear the voice of the Son of God and those who hear will live" (John 5:24).

Jesus is clearly stating that His words give spiritual life, and believing them is necessary for eternal life. His words are not something we can easily dismiss. They don't leave room to stand comfortably on the sidelines. Either you believe Him, or you don't. What about you? How have you responded to Jesus's instruction?

John records the apostle Peter's response: "Simon Peter answered Him, 'Lord, to whom shall we go? You have the words of eternal life. We have come to believe and to know that you are the Holy One of God'" (John 6:68-69).

Peter saw Jesus activate the natural to the supernatural just by His words. If we follow John's Gospel, we know when Peter made this statement. He had seen water turned to wine, an official's son healed in another town, and a 38-year-old man, lame from birth, get up and walk. He'd witnessed the blind seeing, five thousand people fed with a few loaves and fishes, and Jesus walking on water. As their journey with Jesus continued, Peter and the other disciples would see Jesus stop a hurricane, cast out demons, and raise Lazarus from the dead, all through the power of His words. Jesus didn't just make statements; He backed up what He said by powerful, life-giving miracles. Even though Peter didn't understand it all, he knew these were words of life.

As I have studied the Gospels, identifying the commands of Jesus, I have been chagrined in my spirit. Thinking back to my ordination, the elders laid hands on me and quoted the Great Commission: "Go make disciples teaching them to obey everything that I have commanded you" (Matthew 28:19-20). Even though these powerful, life-giving words were given to me at my ordination, this study has caused me to ask myself: Why didn't I do this long ago? What was I thinking? What expert was I listening to about how to teach and preach? Others in my generation and I have opted for different tools, methods, and messages. I'm just now discovering the commands of Jesus that I am to recognize, observe, obey . . . And teach!

The Apostle Paul declared, "For I am not ashamed of the gospel, because it is the power of God that brings salvation to everyone who believes, first the Jew and then the Gentile" (Romans 1:16).

The words of Jesus recorded in the Gospels are the power! Why have we looked for another way to save lost people and build up the church apart from the life-giving, life-changing words of Jesus?

The early apostles knew it, they got it, and they saw with their own eyes what happened when they just told the story and shared those words of Jesus. When Luke wrote the book of Acts, he described the expansion of the early church, saying, "But the word of God continued to spread and flourish" (Acts 12:24).

As I consider the church today, it sometimes seems it's declining, failing, and shrinking. Instead of flourishing, it is dying on the vine. We should not be surprised by this. When we are not obedient to the words of Jesus, we cannot expect to experience the power and life He promised.

Many of us learned a song as children that illustrates this point well. A wise man builds his house on the rock, while a foolish man builds it on the sand. Listen to Matthew 7:24-26: "Therefore, everyone who hears these words of mine and puts them into practice is like a wise man who built his house on the rock. The rain came down, the streams rose, and the winds blew and beat against that house, yet it did not fall, because it had its foundation on the rock. But everyone who hears these words of mine and does not put them into practice is like a foolish man who built his house on sand."

What is the rock? Obedience to the words of Jesus. Jesus is challenging us today— we are supposed to be good listeners and active listeners, obeying what He says. It is the only sure foundation to build our life on.

Read: John 12:47-50, Acts 19:20, Romans 10:17

Reflect: Am I actively listening to the words of Jesus? What do I need to put into practice today?

Pray: Jesus, I am often so busy with my own plans that I fail to hear Your words. Help me to have open ears that are ready to listen. Show me how to put Your words into practice.

CHAPTER 11

Always Pray and Never Give Up

Prayer glorifies God, because it puts us in the position of the thirsty and God in the position of the all-supplying fountain. —John Piper

When I (Stacey) hear the phrase "the squeaky wheel gets the grease," it immediately brings to mind the times when my wife sends me to the grocery store. On such trips, my goal is always efficiency. I go in, and I go out, no wasted motion, no wasted effort. I don't go to extra aisles; I don't peruse; I am not looking for random things; I know exactly where I am going. The best trips to the grocery store for me are the ones when no one even knows I was there.

Maybe it is one of God's ways to keep me humble, but it seems I always choose the worst shopping cart in the store. After adding a few items, that one wheel starts to squeak. Then it shimmies and shakes, and the cart begins to careen, run into other carts, and knock stuff off the shelves. People four aisles away know that I'm coming, and I feel like the whole store is staring at me. An introvert's nightmare!

Despite my embarrassment each time this occurs, I believe that incessant noise from the broken wheel has something to teach us about prayer. In Luke 18:1, Jesus told his disciples to pray and never give up.

> **"One day Jesus told his disciples a story to show that they should always pray and never give up." Luke 18:1**

As He often did, Jesus told a parable to illustrate this truth. He said, "There was a judge in a certain city, who neither feared God nor cared about people. A widow of that city came to him repeatedly, saying, 'Give me justice in this dispute with my enemy.' But the judge ignored her for a while but finally he said to himself, 'I don't fear God or care about people, but this woman is driving me crazy. I'm going to see that she gets justice, because she is wearing me out with her constant requests!'" (Luke 18:2-6).

I have to be honest and tell you my prayer life is not without frustrations and questions. There are times I poured into prayer with every fiber of my being, even times when I would have wanted God to answer for someone else's benefit, not my own, and too many times those prayers felt like they received no answer at all.

In this passage, Jesus seems to be revealing that it's not enough to simply pray, but somehow in God's economy, how much we pray or how many times we ask might make all the difference. In some profound way, our determination in prayer matters. Through the widow in this story and the squeaky wheel on my shopping cart, God is speaking to you and me, saying, *Be incessant, make your requests continually, constantly, day after day, night after night, and never stop asking God until He reveals an answer.*

One question on the forefront of my mind as I studied these words of Jesus was, "Why?" In Matthew 6:8, Jesus explains that our Father knows exactly what we need even before we ask Him. If God already knows everything, then why is it necessary for me to vocalize and speak my prayer requests at all?

Like us, Jesus's disciples may have sat in silence, dumbfounded at the message He was sharing. Jesus ended His lesson about the persistent widow with these clarifying words: "Then the Lord said, 'Learn a lesson from this unjust judge. Even he rendered a decision in the end. So, don't you think God will surely give justice to his chosen people who cry out to him day and night? Will he keep putting them off?'" (Luke 18:6).

Here, Jesus illustrates two completely different ends of the spectrum. On the one hand, you have a sinful judge who acts out of annoyance at the many requests of the woman. But on the other side, you have a Heavenly Father who answers out of a heart of great love and affection.

When I think about the seasons that I've felt the closest to God, almost without exception, it has been during seasons of hardship and pain. I believe that God uses blessing and comfort to try and draw us in and keep us close; however, too often, I've mistaken God's blessing for my own handiwork, which has resulted in drifting away into smug self-reliance. On the other hand, my seasons of helplessness, need, emptiness, lack of peace, and powerlessness have routinely moved me back to my knees.

Friends, we cannot miss the importance of this humble attitude of faith, trust, and reliance on God. It would be easy to complain about why He would go to such lengths to keep us dependent. That is until we remember that it is only by faith, trust, and reliance that any of us are saved. When we question God's willingness to answer our prayers in our time of great need, we have to remember He loves us enough that He willingly chose to send His Son to die for us.

I wonder if someone reading these words is on the verge of giving up on prayer. Maybe you have been praying and praying for a long time, weeks, months, or years for some prayer request that is so very important and critical in your life. I urge you, please don't quit. Jesus Himself is instructing you today that God is listening and God cares deeply for the things you are praying for. I don't know if His answer will come now or in eternity. But I do know that He will answer.

If the devil has convinced you that you are not good enough to ask God for help, believer, please remember that the devil is a liar. Jesus loves you; He has given His very best on your behalf. Listen to the words in Romans 5:8: "But God showed his great love for us by sending Christ to die for us while we were still sinners."

Often, we allow our pride to hold us back from praying. In James 4:2, we are reminded, "You do not have because you do not ask God." Friend, God loves you, and if pride is holding you back, keeping you from bending and bowing your head before Almighty God and asking Him, then please consider getting down off of the pedestal that this world has placed you on, that you have placed you on. Fall down on your knees before God in humble prayer and seek Him with all your heart before it's too late.

If you are discouraged in prayer, please remember the words of David: "Yet I am confident I will see the Lord's goodness while I am here in the land of the living. Wait patiently for the Lord. Be brave and courageous. Yes, wait patiently for the Lord" (Psalm 27:13).

Read: Psalm 121:1-8, Ephesians 6:18, John 15:5, Proverbs 15:29

Reflect: Do I believe that God hears and answers my prayers?

Pray: God, thank You for inviting us to present our requests to You, not just one time but over and over again. Help me to be like the persistent widow who didn't give up until she received an answer.

CHAPTER 12

PRACTICE SECRECY

In the discipline of secrecy, we abstain from causing our good deeds and qualities to be known, we may even take steps to prevent them from being known. We learn to love to be unknown and even to accept misunderstanding without the loss of our peace, joy and purpose. We allow God to decide when our deeds will be known and when our light will be noticed.
—Dallas Willard, *The Spirit of the Disciplines*

I (Todd) grew up a preacher's kid. We didn't have much money, and I always wore hand-me-downs. One year, when I was probably about eight, my mom took me shopping for my first pair of new blue jeans and a brand-new pair of black dress shoes. I was thrilled. I asked my mom to buy me polish for my shoes. Do you remember the bottles of liquid polish with the sponge applicator? Even though she was concerned I would make a mess, she reluctantly agreed.

As soon as I got home, I took my treasures up to my bedroom and polished those brand-new shoes. Then, I set the polish down—with the cap off—and ran off to play. I returned to find that the polish had fallen over onto those brand-new jeans and had spread a huge black spot on them. I panicked, put them on a hanger, and hung them in the furthest back recess of my closet. For a year and a half, I lived in dread and fear every day that those jeans were going to be discovered.

Then, it happened. One day, I came home from school, and my mom was doing laundry. She called out, "Hey Todd, come in here, guess what I found!" I walked in there terrified. My mom was holding a pair of jeans, "Look at these; these were in your closet. Did you forget about these jeans?" I stood there speechless as she said, "Strangest thing, there was this black spot, but I washed them, and it came right out. Try them on." I did... and they were too small. I never got to wear those jeans. What a waste!

There is a sermon illustration here about the black spots and hidden sins in our lives, but that isn't why I'm telling this story. I shared it because we're going to talk about secrecy. Jesus instructed that when we pray, we are to go into our closet, shut the door, and pray. I want to testify that as a little boy, I went into that closet, I knelt among the shoes, and poured my heart out that my new ruined jeans wouldn't be found!

About halfway through the Sermon on the Mount, Jesus introduces the idea of secrecy and gives us three areas to practice it.

> **"Be careful not to practice your righteousness in front of others to be seen by them. If you do, you will have no reward from your Father in Heaven. So when you give to the needy, do not announce it with trumpets, as the hypocrites do in the synagogues and on the streets, to be honored by others. Truly I tell you, they have received their reward in full."**
> **Matthew 6:1-2**

First, we are commanded to have secrecy in our giving. Jesus even adds a little humor to His instructions: "Don't even let your left hand know what your right hand is doing" (Matthew 6:3). While this is impossible to implement, Jesus is making a point about just how secret we should be.

However, earlier in the same sermon, Jesus seems to contradict Himself when He says, "In this same way, let your light shine before others, that they may see your good deeds and glorify your Father in Heaven" (Matthew 5:16). Wait, which is it? Are we not to let people see our deeds so that our Father, who sees them in secret, can reward us? Or are we to let people see our good deeds so we can bring glory to God?

Jesus's original audience would have understood that He was contrasting the kind of giving He desired from the kind of public show the people were used to seeing from their religious leaders, particularly the Pharisees. The Pharisees would make a parade of bringing their tithes and offerings to the synagogue, with their servants carrying bags of coins and hired trumpet players drawing attention.

Humility is key to understanding this teaching on secrecy. When you practice your giving in front of others to be seen by them, it negates your offering. No matter how large it is, no matter what kind of sacrifice it is, if you give it in a way to draw attention to yourself rather than give glory to God, you have received payment in full—the admiration of others. But if you give it secretly, you will receive a reward from our Heavenly Father. I believe there are temporal earthly advantages and rewards from God when we give to others. But I also think there's some kind of heavenly deposit made in our account when we do things that only God sees, the treasures in Heaven Jesus teaches us about.

Next, Jesus teaches us about the secrecy of prayer. "And when you pray, do not be like the hypocrites, for they love to pray standing in the synagogues and on the street corners to be seen by others. Truly I tell you, they have received their reward in full. But when you pray, go into your room, close the door and pray to your Father, who is unseen. Then your Father, who sees what is done in secret, will reward you" (Matthew 6:5-7).

The Pharisees loved to pray out in the open or in a prominent place in the temple with grandiose, dramatic, long prayers and big words. Jesus said not to pray like that because these hypocrites are paid in full through the notice and adoration of others.

Instead, we are to pray secret prayers, only heard by God Himself in a secret place. The King James version translates the word for "secret" here as "closet," and some people have taken that quite literally, crawling into the closet among the clothes and shoes, like I did as a little boy. But the idea here is actually an "inner room" or quiet space. I am pretty sure my mom's secret place, like a lot of mothers, was the bathroom—the one place she could get alone and beg God for help. Do you have an inner room, an inner sanctum, some quiet place that has been made holy because that's where God sees you and hears you and rewards you in secrecy?

Let's be clear: Jesus is not telling us we should not pray corporately. The Bible gives many examples of the church praying together, but that should never replace the rich experience of private prayers. I have to confess to you that there are days when the only time I pray is when somebody calls on me to pray or at mealtime. When I don't always make time for the secret prayer in the inner room alone with God, I wonder, what kind of reward am I missing?

Jesus continues with a third command connected to secrecy. "When you fast, do not look somber as the hypocrites do, for they disfigure their faces to show others they are fasting. Truly I tell you, they have received their reward in full" (Matthew 6:16-18).

Today, we hear about the benefits fasting can have on our health, and while those may be true, fasting is intended as a sacrifice to God. When we fast, we are not supposed to announce it to our family or to our coworkers. *Hey, I can't go out to eat with you today, or I'm going to pass on the donuts because I'm fasting today.* The Pharisees fasted to be seen by others. They would put dust on their clothes and put ashes on their head, and they would smear their face with dirt then walk around looking miserable.

Again, Jesus reminds us that our reward comes from our Father, who sees what is done in secret. "But when you fast, put oil on your head and wash your face, so that it will not be obvious to others that you are fasting, but only to your Father, who is unseen; and your Father, who sees what is done in secret, will reward you" (Matthew 6:16-18).

When Jesus repeats something twice, it's important to take note. When He repeats something three times, this is how we should live. When we give, when we pray, when we fast, we are to do it in secret. That is where we find our reward.

Let me conclude with this quote from Michael R. Palmer:

> The discipline of secrecy goes against the current expectations of our culture. Right now the culture expectation is for people to share their whole lives with the world. In every social media post or video we create, we want to be seen, we want to be valued. We want people to see our generosity, our kindness and our support of some particular cause. This impulse is exacerbated by but not limited to social media. The need for public affirmation is close at hand for all of us. We can find it in our telling of stories, where we make ourselves the hero or publicly share our acts of generosity with friends, maybe in a small Bible study together. In reality, our desires and actions can be complicated. So much of what we do is a complicated mixture of true generosity and self-centered desire for affirmation. We want to help others, we do, but our hearts are torn by the desire for people to see what we've done.[12]

Our righteousness is to be practiced for God's eyes only, in the secret place of His presence. Yes, there are times when God will lead us to practice good deeds in a more public setting, but if we are doing so to be seen, it is better to stay at home. We will lose our reward.

Read: Psalm 27:4-5, Isaiah 58, Luke 18:16-18, 2 Corinthians 9:7

Reflect: Do you need to reframe how you practice righteousness? Are you hiding in the secret place or are you looking for attention and applause?

Pray: God, I want to talk with You in the secret place—just You and me. Help me to walk in humility, focused on pleasing You and not the people around me. Thank You for allowing me to meet with You, today.

CHAPTER 13

DO THE WILL OF MY FATHER

If we are truly devoted to doing God's will, pain and pleasure won't make any difference to us.   —Brother Lawrence

Recently, I (Todd) was teaching a class on Heaven. I shared this joke:

A guy dies and goes to Heaven. He shows up surprised and works through the fog and the mist until he comes to Saint Peter. Looking over a big book, Peter asks, "What's your name?"

The guy gives his name.

"Date of birth?"

He gives it.

Peter locates the man and says, "Hmm, it looks like you've not done a lot of bad things in your life, and you haven't done a lot of good either. I'm on the fence about letting you in. Is there anything that you've done that's not written down here that might swing me one way or the other?"

The guy responds, "Well, I think so; I was driving downtown, and there was a gang of thugs with knives out circling this little old lady, threatening her to take her purse. I slammed on the brakes and ran over to that circle, broke through, grabbed the leader by the shirt, slapped him, and said, 'you better leave her alone, or you're going to deal with me.'"

Saint Peter said, "Really? That's awesome. By the way, when did that happen?"

The man answered, "about five minutes ago."

This joke humorously (though inaccurately!) looks at the question of who goes to Heaven. A popular theology taught in seminaries and churches worldwide teaches that everybody goes to Heaven. But that is not what God's Word teaches. As we look at Jesus's command to "do the will of My Father," we will see clearly who goes to Heaven and who does not.

We are going to return to the Sermon on the Mount. Let's pick up with Matthew 7, where Jesus warns us to look out for false prophets who look as innocent as sheep but are really wolves in disguise. Ultimately, Jesus explains that we will know these false prophets by their fruit. Good trees bear good fruit, and bad trees bear bad fruit. Distinguishing the false prophets from true believers comes down to this.

Jesus continues,

> **"Not everyone who says to me, 'Lord, Lord,' will enter the kingdom of heaven, but only the one who does the will of my Father who is in heaven."**   **Matthew 7:21**

Jesus then points us to Judgment Day. "Many on that day will say to me, 'Lord, Lord,' did we not prophesy in your name and in your name drive out demons and in your name perform many miracles?' Then I will tell them plainly, 'I never knew you. Away from me, you evildoers!'" (Matthew 7:22-23).

In his letter to the Galatians, Paul's teaching helps us identify both bad and good fruit. He starts with the bad fruit: "The acts of the flesh are obvious: sexual immorality, impurity, debauchery, idolatry and witchcraft, hatred, discord, jealousy, fits of rage, selfish ambition, dissensions, factions and envy, drunkenness, orgies, and the like. I warn you, as I did before, that those who live like this will not inherit the Kingdom of God" (Galatians 5:19-21).

Then Paul turns to the good fruit, reminding the Galatians of the kind of fruit they are to produce, where it comes from, and what it looks like. "But the fruit of the Spirit is love, joy, peace, forbearance, kindness, goodness, faithfulness, gentleness and self-control" (Galatians 5:22-23). When we are saved by God's grace, we are filled with His Spirit and bear good fruit by doing the will of our Father in Heaven.

Let's look at another time Jesus talks about doing the will of His Father. I'll be honest: On a first read, Jesus could come off as a little haughty, maybe even snotty! You'll see what I mean.

Jesus is talking to a crowd, and someone alerts Him that His mother and brothers are waiting to speak to Him. Jesus responds, "Who is my mother and my brothers? For whoever does the will of my Father in Heaven is my brother and sister and mother" (Matthew 12:49-50).

While it may seem like Jesus is being callous toward His family, He is actually making a beautiful point. Who is a child of God? Anyone who does the will of the Father. If we do the will of the Father, we are His family. We are the brothers, sisters, and mothers of Jesus. Isn't that amazing?

One of my favorite verses is 1 John 3:1: "See what a great love the Father has lavished on us that we should be called children of God!" We are children adopted, invited to the table, born of the King. What a great gift that has been given to us.

As the children of God, we are to do the will of the Father with intentionality and passion. Though not exhaustive, here are four points from Scripture that tell us precisely what is the will of the Father:

1. IT'S THE WILL OF THE FATHER THAT WE ARE SAVED.

In John 6:40, Jesus said, "For my Father's will is that everyone who looks to the Son and believes in him shall have eternal life, and I will raise them up at the last day." It is God's will to save lost people. That the great desire of God is to send people to Hell is a false notion.

Remember John 3:16? "For God so loved the world that He gave His only begotten Son, that whoever would believe in Him wouldn't perish." It's God's will to save us—to save you and to raise you up on the last day.

2. IT IS GOD'S WILL THAT WE LIVE HOLY LIVES.

In 1 Thessalonians 4:3-5, Paul says, "It is God's will that you should be sanctified: that you should avoid sexual immorality; that each of you should learn to control your own body in a way that is holy and honorable, not in passionate lust like the pagans, who do not know God."

We need to take a spiritual inventory of our lives. It is God's will that we are sanctified, set apart, and remain sexually pure. Paul continues with these strong words in verses 7-8: "For God did not call us to be impure, but to live a holy life. Therefore, anyone who rejects this instruction does not reject a human being but God, the very God who gives you his Holy Spirit."

3. IT IS GOD'S WILL THAT WE DO GOOD DEEDS.

In I Peter 2:12, Peter writes, "Live such good lives among the pagans that though they accuse you of doing wrong, they may see your good deeds and glorify God on the day he visits us." He continues in verse 15, "For it is God's will that by doing good you should silence the ignorant talk of foolish people."

We are to do good and live out our faith with actions. It is God's will that we utilize our spiritual gifts and find our place of service in the church and the community.

4. IT IS GOD'S WILL THAT WE LIVE LIVES OF THANKSGIVING ALL THE TIME.

I Thessalonians 5:18 says, "Give thanks in all circumstances; for this is God's will for you in Christ Jesus." It's easy to give thanks and lift your hands in praise on good days when you have health and bounty. But it's nearly impossible to give thanks when the sky has crashed on you and the storm is raging all about. But we are called to give thanks in every situation, even the darkest of all. Paul goes as far as to say that it's God's will.

As you can imagine, in years of ministry, I have journeyed with people through impossibly heart-breaking times, and I secretly privately think to myself, how do I thank God in this situation? One of those times was a visit with a dying man who was in constant pain, to the point it hurt him to speak. After I finished praying over him with the elders of our church, the man said something that bolstered my faith. He whispered, "Gentlemen, God has a plan for me." He trusted that his Heavenly Father had a plan, and then, in a couple of days, he was deceased. That saint had learned to trust God at every stormy turn. Even on his deathbed, he gave praise to God. It's not easy, but with the help of the Holy Spirit, we can do God's will by giving thanks in every situation.

Good fruit is always the result of being close to God and walking with Him. We cannot be intimate with Jesus without doing His will and bearing good fruit. And when we do the will of our Father, we will enter the Kingdom of Heaven and spend all eternity with Him.

Do the Will of My Father

Read: John 15:8, Romans 12:1-2, Ephesians 5:17-21, James 4:13-17

Reflect: What fruit is my life producing? Am I doing the will of my Father in Heaven?

Pray: God, thank You for saving me. Help me to live a life that is focused on Your will, not mine. I surrender my past, present, and future to You for Your glory.

CHAPTER 14

BE READY. WATCH AND WAIT

The doctrine of the Second Coming is deeply uncongenial to the whole evolutionary or developmental character of modern thought. We have been taught to think of the world as something that grows slowly towards perfection, something that "progresses" or "evolves." Christian Apocalyptic offers no such hope. It does not even foretell... a gradual decay. It foretells a sudden, violent end imposed from without; an extinguisher popped onto the candle, a brick flung at the gramophone, a curtain rung down on the play— "Halt!"
—C. S. Lewis

One Sunday over 40 years ago, I (Todd) was teaching children's church in King, North Carolina, where Karen and I were leading youth ministry. The story for that morning was Jesus's ascension when He said goodbye to His disciples and was lifted up to Heaven. As I was talking, a little boy about seven years old named Jason started pounding his head and crying out, "I hate this story, I hate it, please don't tell it."

Not sure what else to do, I asked him, "Why do you hate this story?"

Jason responded, "They let Him get away; why didn't they go for His feet?"

Now that has some serious theological implications, doesn't it? What if the disciples were actually able to keep Jesus here?

Every time I remember Jason's response, although it was cute, I am moved by the intensity of his feelings. Jason didn't want Jesus to leave; he wanted Jesus here with him. I wonder if we feel that same intensity and longing to have Jesus with us.

Of course, we know the disciples could not keep Jesus here on earth; He did leave. He ascended into Heaven with a promise that He would be returning one day. And that promise comes with a command: We, His children, are to be watching and waiting, ready for His return.

> **"Therefore, keep watch because you do not know when the owner of the house will come back—whether in the evening, or at midnight, or when the rooster crows, or at dawn. If he comes suddenly, do not let him find you sleeping. What I say to you, I say to everyone: Watch!"   Mark 13:35-37**

Are you familiar with the children's song "Give Me Oil in My Lamp"? While many of us sang that song as children, most of us had very little idea what we were singing about. The lyrics go something like this: *Give me oil in my lamp, keep me burning, burning, burning, give me oil in my lamp, I pray. Give me oil in my lamp, keep me burning, burning, burning, keep me burning till the break of day.*

This song refers to a story Jesus told His disciples to teach them to be ready for His return. Listen to Luke's account: "Be dressed ready for service and keep your lamps burning, like servants waiting for their master to return from a wedding banquet, so that when he comes and knocks they can immediately open the door for him" (Luke 12:35-36). He goes on to explain that no one knows when the master will return, and it is good for the servant whose master finds them ready. But it is detrimental for the servants who are caught unaware.

In Jesus's day, Jewish weddings lasted a week or more. After the ceremony, the bride and groom went off on their honeymoon. Then, they returned to a room left ready in the groom's father's house, where they took up residence. Often, families would play a game where the bride and groom tried to sneak back into town unnoticed while guests were positioned throughout the town watching, waiting, and even staying up through the night to catch them.

In Matthew 25, Jesus tells the story of ten virgins, all bridesmaids in a wedding. They went out to meet the bridegroom, who took a long time to return. Only five were prepared with enough oil in their lamps for the long wait. Those five joined the wedding banquet, but the remaining five, who ran out of oil, were shut outside, unable to enter.

When Jesus returns, it won't be on a silent night in some obscure village as a baby in a manger. He is coming back riding on the clouds of Heaven with the army of Heaven with Him. Scripture uses various titles for His return, such as The Day of the Lord, The Lord's Day, or the Day of God's Wrath. We often call it the Second Coming.

The Apostle Peter was there for the ascension, gazing up into Heaven until he saw Jesus disappear like a speck into the clouds. Some years later, he would write to the early church, which was growing weary and even skeptical about the Lord's return:

> But do not forget this one thing, dear friends: With the Lord a day is like a thousand years, and a thousand years like a day. The Lord is not slow in keeping his promise as some understand slowness. Instead, he is patient with you, not wanting anyone to perish, but everyone to come to repentance. But the day of the Lord will come like a thief. The heavens will disappear with a roar; the elements will be destroyed by fire and the earth and everything done in it will be laid bare. Since everything will be destroyed in this way, what kind of people ought you to be? We ought to live holy and godly lives as you look forward to the day of God and speed its coming. (2 Peter 3:8-12)

Did you notice that last part? Really? Can we speed the Lord's coming? Or, as one translation says, hasten it? The prayer of the early church was Lord Jesus: come quickly, hurry up, come back! What about you? Do you want it to happen? Do you want Him to come back? Today? Soon?

Philippians 3:20-21 reminds us, "But our citizenship is in Heaven. And we eagerly await a Savior from there, the Lord Jesus Christ, who, by the power that enables him to bring everything under his control, will transform our lowly bodies so that they will be like his glorious body."

We are to be ready, watching, waiting, with oil in our lamps. If Jesus were speaking to us today, He'd say, keep your batteries charged, keep your flashlight close by, and keep your phone with you.

I hope we can all honestly say these words with Paul, "I have fought the good fight, I have finished the race, I have kept the faith. Now there is in store for me the crown of righteousness, which the Lord, the righteous Judge will award to me on that day- and not only to me, but also to all who have longed for his appearing" (2 Timothy 4:7-8).

Read: Luke 12:35-48, Acts 1:9-11, Romans 8:23, I Thessalonians 5:1-11, Titus 2:11-14, Revelation 1:7

Reflect: Am I eagerly watching and waiting for Jesus's return? Am I ready?

Pray: Come quickly, Jesus. We look forward to the day when You come back. Help us to be faithful servants, ready for Your return.

SECTION 3

THE HARD STUFF

On hearing it, many of his disciples said, "This is a hard teaching. Who can accept it?"

John 6:60

CHAPTER 15

FEAR HIM WHO CAN DESTROY BOTH BODY AND SOUL

> *There is no doctrine which I would more willingly remove from Christianity than the doctrine of Hell, if it lay in my power. But it has the support of Scripture and especially, of our Lord's own words; it has always been held by the Christian Church, and it has the support of reason.*
> —C. S. Lewis

There are a lot of bothersome things in the Bible—tough teachings that we either want to get by real fast or that just don't make sense to us. Like these words of Jesus, "If someone hits you on one side of the face, turn the other cheek and let them hit that side as well." That personally bothers me (Todd). Or "Be perfect even as your Heavenly Father is perfect." That one's challenging, isn't it?

Theologians write reams about what these things mean. My guess is that there is a straightforward explanation if we just look at it plainly and simply. But they're still bothersome. And we can't put our heads in the sand about these hard biblical truths that we know are there but we just don't want to acknowledge. I love this quote by Mark Twain: "It ain't the parts of the Bible that I can't understand that bother me; it is the parts that I do understand."[13]

Many Christians ignore some pretty basic and pretty important simple truths of the Bible. Worse than that, many pastors and teachers have stopped teaching things that are unpleasant and uncomfortable. One of those unpleasant truths is the Bible's teaching on Hell. The Bible contains some very straightforward, descriptive, and even fearsome images of

Hell. It's described with terms like outer darkness, a fiery lake, a blazing furnace, a place where the worm never dies, a place of punishment for the wicked where they are thrown together with Satan and demons!

Pretty scary, isn't it? In fact, Jesus commands us to be afraid:

> **"Do not be afraid of those who kill the body but cannot kill the soul. Rather, be afraid of the One who can destroy both soul and body in Hell."** **Matthew 10:28**

Who is the "One" mentioned here? It might surprise you to learn it is not the devil. Contrary to cartoons and cultural belief, Satan is not in Hell sitting on a fiery throne commanding his demons. It's the last place he wants to be. He will fight until his last breath to escape it. No, the "One" Jesus is talking about is His Heavenly Father.

Jesus, the only begotten, present with God since the beginning of time, knew all about God's patient mercy and divine justice. He stood by His Father when the fountains of the deep burst forth and the wicked were destroyed in the days of Noah.

Some of the most jarring descriptions of Hell come from Jesus Himself. Seven times in the Gospels, He refers to Hell with these words, "It is a place of outer darkness, a place of weeping and gnashing of teeth." John Piper helps us understand that description from Jesus with these words, "In other words, all the joys that we associate with light will be withdrawn, and all the fears that we associate with darkness will be multiplied. And the result will be an intensity of misery that makes a person grind his teeth in order to bear it."[14]

Jesus's own apostles did not mince words themselves about the coming wrath of God. Peter wrote, "The Lord knows how to rescue the godly from trials and to hold the unrighteous for punishment on the Day of Judgement. This is especially true of those who follow the corrupt desires of the flesh and despise authority" (II Peter 2:9-10).

In Revelation 19:11-21, John records the terrifying events of the Lord's return. He sees the skies part and the Lord Jesus descend from Heaven with the armies of Heaven, who, by the way, are the risen saints coming back with Him in power and authority. The wicked on that day are destroyed with a supernatural sword from the mouth of Jesus. Others are thrown, alive, into "the fiery lake of burning sulfur." John's account is straightforward: This is not fable; it's just John's vision, a record of what he saw.

While God is a just and righteous judge who has promised in His Word that there is a day of wrath coming upon the world, He is also the Savior, the merciful King of the universe.

The prophet Daniel, living as an exile in Babylon, centuries before Jesus, would have a vision of that Day of Judgment, the Day of the Lord, the resurrection of the dead and he put that vision to pen. He wrote in Daniel 12: "Multitudes who sleep in the dust of the earth will awake; some to everlasting life, others to shame and everlasting contempt. Those who are wise will shine like the brightness of the heavens, and those who lead many to righteousness, like the stars for ever and ever" (Daniel 12:2-3).

There are many people in the world who never think about walking into church, never think about calling themselves a Christian, who want to believe that Heaven is for real — that when they die, regardless of how they've lived, they are going straight there, and they embrace that hope enthusiastically. While many are embracing the idea of Heaven, more and more Christians are accepting a false notion that Hell just doesn't exist, just couldn't exist.

As Christians, we long for Christ's return. We believe that when Christ returns, there will be a great trumpet blast, the voice of the archangel and the dead in Christ will rise, and we will receive our rewards and be ushered into the Kingdom. There will be a great and glad reunion with our loved ones who have died in faith before us. Yet, from the Old Testament prophets to the Apostle John in Revelation is recorded the sobering reality that the Son of Man is coming in great power to exact vengeance upon the wicked, to rescue the saved, and to judge the wicked.

Rather than obeying Christ's commands and accepting His offer of rescue, there is a generation of Christians who have chosen to believe a doctrine of Hell based on a popular, yet godless song written by John Lennon, "Imagine." These are the opening words of that song: "Imagine there's no Heaven, it's easy if you try, no Hell below us, above us only sky. Imagine all the people living for today."

Living for today, is the definition of hedonism. Doing what you want. Choosing what you want reality to be. Deciding there's no Heaven and no Hell.

If I am honest, like C. S. Lewis, I'd love to relieve us all of that horrible certainty. I don't want to think of that dark place of eternal torment and suffering. It has and does at times challenge me to find the balance between God's mercy and His wrath. But it's true. It's all true.

Jesus knew this: Hell is real. Listen to how He describes the impact of following Him: "Very truly I tell you, whoever hears my word and believes Him who sent me has eternal life and will not be judged but has crossed over from death to life" (John 5:24).

The book of Titus also explains our need for a Savior: "But when the kindness and love of God our Savior appeared, he saved us, not because of the righteous things we had done but because of his mercy. He saved us through the washing of rebirth and renewal by the Holy Spirit, whom he poured out on us generously through Jesus Christ our Savior" (Titus 3:4-6).

Did you hear those words? Mercy, given generously, poured out. But why? Because He needed to save us.

If we truly believe in Jesus and follow His teachings, we cannot avoid the reality of Hell. We can only accept His mercy and salvation and share the Good News with others.

Read: John 5:28, Matthew 5:22, 29, Matthew 25:41, Luke 16:19-31, Matthew 13:24-50

Reflect: What do you believe about Hell? Do you struggle with accepting its existence?

Pray: Father, thank You for Your mercy. Reflecting on Hell is sobering, but it also reminds us of the deep love and sacrifice of Jesus our Savior.

CHAPTER 16

ENTER THROUGH THE NARROW DOOR

There is a way that seems right to a man, but its end is the way to death.   *—King Solomon*

In Luke 13, we find another command of Jesus that must have caught people by surprise when He said it.

> **"Make every effort to enter through the narrow door, because many, I tell you, will try to enter and will not be able to."**
> **Luke 13:24**

What a cryptic statement, what an interesting thing to say to a crowd of people. What is this narrow way? What is this door that we must enter through?

Friends, the idea that there is only one way, a narrow door to God, is a hard truth for someone like me (Stacey), born in the United States, a nation born of trailblazers, pioneers, and explorers. With independence and freedom comes the expectation of control. We like to be the master of our destiny. We want to steer and determine our own direction, even if that direction leads us to failure and destruction.

Much of the free western world has popularized the idea that many roads lead to God. Intellectuals and scholars claim that all religions are essentially the same with only superficial differences. For example, Abhishek Singh, who leads a large international organization called "The Planetary Development Institute," writes, "Whether anyone goes to a temple, a church, or a mosque, they are all the same. Whether you pray to Jesus or Allah or meditate on Buddha the results will be similar. Therefore, adherence of all religious trends should live happily together recognizing there is no real conflict in what they believe. Because the differences lie only at the level of surface variations and name and form."[15]

How well do you think that statement would go over at a local mosque? Do you think you can convince a Hindu, Buddhist, Mormon, or Satanist that we are all on the same journey with only superficial differences? The truth of the matter is that all of the world's religions are fundamentally different, with only superficial similarities. All religions are not the same road, and Jesus is making clear that all roads do not lead to God.

When He speaks of the narrow door, Jesus paints a picture of somewhere difficult to access. He tells us to make every effort to enter, or as some versions translate, to "strive to enter." The word *strive* that Jesus uses means *to agonize, struggle, or contend in intense warfare or athletic preparation and competition.*[16]

I still remember high school football like it was yesterday. I grew up in a small farming community in New York State and didn't have the opportunity to play Little League sports until I moved to Virginia, so my sophomore year in high school was my first time on a real football field. One practice day in August was what our team called "Oklahoma,"—the first day of full contact. I didn't know exactly what was coming, but as I watched everyone getting amped up, I had a feeling it would be bad.

Kids were growling; the coaches were taking players by the facemask and encouraging them to pound somebody! Then, the coaches selected five "sacrificial lambs" to line up in front of the rest of team. I was one of those chosen and placed in front of an upperclassman named Eric Meadows. Eric was one of the most kindhearted and wonderful people in our school, but when he put on his football helmet, something changed in his personality. I can still remember him running in place, drooling out of one side of his mouth, mumbling words no one can understand. Then, to make it worse, the coach grabs him by the face mask and says, "Just kill them, Eric, just kill them!" And there I am, standing at 135 pounds with only a little yellow pad in my hands for protection.

The coach blew the whistle, and Eric came flying at me a hundred miles an hour, lifted me up by the thighs, and buried me in the ground with all his might. All the air went out of my lungs, and the only thing I really remember is pain and thinking, "Thank the Lord this is over." Then the coach stands me up and says, "Burkholder, get your pad up!" It was then I realized that I wasn't finished. The whistle blew, and here comes the next guy. Then again and again.

It was there in the dirt and dust of that practice field, that I first learned what it meant to strive. I look back on those days and think about the lessons I learned agonizing and battling all to get time on the actual playing field during the game.

I wonder if this is the Gospel message you received about what it would be like to follow Jesus—a narrow way of agonizing blood, sweat, tears, and effort. The Apostle Paul understood this very well when he wrote in I Corinthians 9:27 NLT, "I discipline my body like an athlete, training it to do what it should. Otherwise, I fear that after preaching to others I myself might be disqualified."

Can't you picture the Apostle Paul on his harrowing journey grizzled and scarred, Bible in one hand, torch in the other, going from town to town, demons dragging off of his ankles as he kicked them aside and went on, one more day in obedience to Christ? In 2 Corinthians 11, Paul gives us a snapshot of what his narrow path was filled with: 39 lashes, beaten with rods, stoned, shipwrecked, long journeys, robbers, sleepless nights, hungry and thirsty, lack of clothing, attacked by both Jews and Gentiles.

Is that the type of journey you expect to walk with Jesus Christ? Friends, Jesus invites us to step away from the path the world is walking and instead join Him on the more difficult and narrow way. This way will require striving, agonizing, and great effort. However, the striving leads to an unsurpassed and wonderful reward in this life and the next, especially when compared with the trinkets and garbage that this world has to offer.

Now, let's slow down for just a minute in all this striving and sweat and identify what we are striving for. When Jesus commands us to strive to enter through the narrow door or gate, what is this gate? There was another conversation that Jesus had with His disciples when He clarified what He was referring to when He preached about this mysterious entrance. "I am the gate; whoever enters through me will be saved. They will come in and go out, and find pasture. The thief comes only to steal and kill and destroy; I have come that they may have life, and have it to the full" (John 10:9-10).

Jesus Christ, God in the flesh, is the only way to Heaven. Right before Jesus was crucified, He gathered His disciples and told them He was going to go away to prepare a place for them. Thomas was bewildered and confused and asked the question the rest of them probably wanted to ask, "Lord, we don't know where you are going, so how can we know the way?" (John 14:5).

Jesus answers with this profound statement, "I am the way and the truth and the life. No one comes to the Father except through me" (John 14:6). You might be surprised to learn that the original Greek word that Jesus uses here for "no one" means no one. Jesus is speaking straight to you and me today and revealing in no uncertain terms that in this life, there are not many paths to God, only one.

I would like to humbly ask you to look inside your own heart and life and ask yourself: Are you striving? Are you agonizing, struggling, and contending in intense effort to remain on this narrow path that God has placed before us?

I can speak from personal experience about living life on the broad path. There is nothing there but empty promises, empty victories, and lost and wandering people seeking purpose and meaning. If you are walking on that wide, easy path today, please know if you will turn from your sin, if you look to the cross of Jesus Christ, you will find peace, purpose, love, and joy unsurpassed by anything this world can offer.

Read: Matthew 7:13-14, Luke 9:57-62, Philippians 3:13-14

Reflect: Are you striving to remain on the narrow path? Or are you wandering down the wide path?

Pray: Jesus, thank You for making a way to God through Your death on the cross. I acknowledge You are the only way and choose to strive to walk on the narrow way.

CHAPTER 17

DO NOT LUST

The most important thing to remember as we talk about sexual purity is this: God is for you! God wants you to win.
—*Sam Storms*

Have you ever found yourself asking the question, how did I get here? Maybe you've opened up your credit card statement and wondered how it got this bad. You think surely someone got my credit card number and spent without my permission. Or maybe you've stood in front of an attorney, a judge, a parent, or a spouse with your decisions laid out before you like that credit card statement, pointing to one thing after another that led to the mess your life has become.

When I (Stacey) was in student ministry, I received a late-night phone call that I will never forget. On the other end was a mom asking me to come over to her house. She couldn't explain what happened over the phone, but I knew by the way her voice cracked and quivered, something terrible had happened. When I arrived at the house, the tearful mom led me to the living room, where the 14-year-old daughter sat, head down. After a few minutes, the mom revealed that her daughter had confided for the very first time that she had been molested by her father for over a year. It is hard to grasp what that realization would feel like landing on the heart of a mom, walking through what to do, whom to call, and where to turn.

Before long, the police arrived. Because the parents were divorced, two police left shortly to go to the father's house, only a few miles away. Can you imagine that knock on the door? For the first time, the realization, the full realization, the snowball effect of decisions that now crashed on his front porch as he was handcuffed and taken away.

That night, back at the home with the mother and daughter, there was no celebration, no sense of victory at the father's arrest. Instead, that night represented so much loss. The loss of integrity, the loss of innocence, the loss of trust, the loss of freedom. I've wondered what it must have been like as that man sits behind bars, his life shattered. Does he ask himself: How did I get here? How did it ever get so bad?

While I don't claim to understand what goes through the heart and mind of someone that could enact such cruelty on a child, what I can say for certain is that somewhere in the earliest stages of this tragedy, there was a moment when normal love and affection was exchanged for lust. The subtle beginning of lust is like a seed waiting in our hearts. If the tiny seed of lust that lies buried in our hearts is starved and neglected, it will remain small. However, when that seed is nourished and nurtured, it will begin to grow and take root in a powerful way.

Jesus didn't shy away from these types of hard topics when He taught. Imagine the looks on the faces of the people listening when Jesus shared this command:

> **"You have heard that it was said, 'You shall not commit adultery.' But I tell you that anyone who looks at a woman lustfully has already committed adultery with her in his heart."**
> **Matthew 5:27-28**

For some reason, we've begun trivializing lust as some rite of passage that every child must go through. Pornography use is written off as just a part of growing up, and parents now provide contraception for their children so they can safely engage in sexual activity. The culture of lust and perversion that is being driven by powerful social media is not just restricted to our children, but it impacts every sector of our society. We should be shocked to find out that those very same sins aren't just rampant in the general population but amongst ministry professionals. Unfortunately, we have become so accustomed to the reality of lust and sexual sin in our public life that we barely blink an eye, even in the church.

The worldwide porn industry, according to many statistics that I have read, will have a greater revenue this year than the NFL, NBA, and NHL combined.[17] What an incredible force just beneath the surface of our lives. While the world celebrates lust and invents darker and more insidious ways of feeding its endless appetite, Jesus continues His warning against lust with these strong words, "If your right eye causes you to stumble, gouge it out and throw it away. It is better for you to lose one part of your body than for your whole body to be thrown into hell. And if your right hand causes you to stumble, cut it off and throw it away. It is better for you to lose one part of your body than for your whole body to go into Hell" (Matthew 5:29-30).

One of the most heartbreaking stories in all of the Bible is that of David's sexual sin. David was the prototype of Biblical bravery and faithfulness and the king over all of Israel, yet at the height of his power, we find him overlooking the city from the roof of his palace. He noticed a woman of unusual beauty taking a bath and sent messengers to get her. I wonder how many times after this event David asked himself, why couldn't she have not been home, why did I send the messenger, why did she answer the door, why did I do this thing?

Those few moments of fleeting pleasure were followed by a series of devastating consequences: David had the husband of Bathsheba murdered. The child conceived in the sinful night of passion died. David's son Amnon allowed his own lust to burn so out of control that he raped his half-sister, Tamar. Absalom, another of David's sons, so angered by what happened to his sister, murdered his brother. Then he decided he now wanted to be king in the place of his father. In a statement of defiance and disrespect to his dad, he took David's concubines onto the palace rooftop and slept with each one of them in view of all Israel. Soon after as a result, Absalom himself would be killed by one of the king's leaders.

Within hours of Absalom's death, we find David heartbroken. 2 Samuel 18:33 details that moment: "The king was shaken. He went up to the room over the gateway and wept. As he went, he said: 'O my son Absalom! My son, my son Absalom! If only I had died instead of you—O Absalom, my son, my son!'"

Friends, the carnage that was wrought in David's life because of his sin was not born on the rooftop. It did not originate from a misplaced glance at a bathing woman. David's undoing was born in a lingering thought, a lasting glance, a growing desire. By the time that seed of lust was revealed in David's life, it had likely been nurtured and fed for weeks, months, or even years in his heart.

The book of James is packed with very direct and hard-hitting truths. Listen as James writes about how lust rears its ugly head in our lives: "Temptation comes from our own desires, which entice us and drag us away. These desires give birth to sinful actions. And when sin is allowed to grow, it gives birth to death" (James 1:14-15). Notice that temptation in each one of our lives is born from our own desires. We can't blame the internet, we can't blame other people, we can't blame the devil himself when we give in to temptation. The only reason we're drawn in is because, deep in our hearts, we already desire it. The temptation would be ineffective if it wasn't something we already craved.

Friends, the Lord is not ignorant of what we do in secret, what we think, or what we bury in our hearts. He sees straight through the façade. It's time we wake up and realize that the world is lying to us, filling our minds and feeding the lust in our hearts with seductive books, movies, and pornographic images. It doesn't matter how many of our friends, coworkers, and families are doing these things. Lust is a deadly, eternal sin and, according to the Word of God, carries a sentence of not only earthly hardship but eternal spiritual death.

To finish this hard conversation, let me remind you that if this topic fills you with guilt and regret, God wants you to know today that you are loved. For any man or woman that has woken up from a one-night stand feeling the weight of guilt and regret, for the spouse that finds their world crashing down after deciding to plunge headlong into an affair, for any teenager that faces the humiliation of indecent pictures of themselves intended for a boyfriend or girlfriend that are instead shared on social media, for the woman faced with an unplanned pregnancy, for the person sneaking through life entangled in the grips of pornography, to each one of these people that have fallen victim to their own lust, God wants you to know today that you are loved. He wants to forgive you, and He wants to redeem and restore your life.

I love this image and invitation from God from Isaiah, "'Come now, let us settle the matter,' says the Lord. 'Though your sins are like scarlet, they shall be as white as snow; though they are red as crimson, they shall be like wool'" (Isaiah 1:18).

Read: Job 31:1-4, Proverbs 4:23, Proverbs 6:27-29, Matthew 6:22-23, 1 Corinthians 9:27

Reflect: Am I nurturing the seed of lust in my heart and mind?

Pray: God, forgive me for feeding lust and evil desires instead of seeking You. Help me to find freedom and victory.

CHAPTER 18

RENDER UNTO CAESAR

> *Show proper respect to everyone, love the family of believers, fear God, honor the emperor.* —Peter, Apostle of Jesus

Let's talk about taxes. Yes, I (Todd) know, a favorite subject for most people. Benjamin Franklin said, "In this world, nothing is certain except for death and taxes."[18] Mark Twain said, "What's the difference between a taxidermist and a tax collector? The taxidermist only takes your skin."[19]

Taxes—collecting taxes, paying taxes, and complaining about taxes—are a big deal for Americans today. And they were a big deal in Jesus's day too when oppressive Rome ruled the world. The Romans had taken over Israel and demanded extraordinary taxes from the people. This oppressive regime that crucified common thieves would certainly not hesitate to crucify someone who didn't pay taxes.

Being a tax collector was one of the most despised careers in Israel. The Jewish people hated their own brethren who had been hired by Rome. Receiving extraordinary kickbacks, they were considered the scum of the earth. You'll remember that Jesus was criticized for eating and drinking with prostitutes, drunkards, and tax collectors. Matthew, whose Gospel account we are going to look at, was a tax collector turned disciple.

In Matthew 17, we find Jesus and the disciples in Jerusalem when someone walks up to Peter and asks, "Hey, does the rabbi pay the temple tax?" In addition to the Roman tax, the Jewish authorities added their own taxes. By law, there was a tax of two drachmas for going into the temple to worship God. Peter quickly responded that yes, Jesus paid His taxes.

Later, Jesus explained to Peter that because He was the Son of God, He was exempt from temple taxes, but He continued, "I tell you what, Peter, so we don't offend anybody, I want you to take your fishing pole and go to the lake, throw your line in, and open the mouth of the first fish you catch, where you'll find four drachmas, and then go pay my tax and yours." And that's what Peter did. That would be a fun way to pay taxes, wouldn't it?

One of the commonly known phrases from the Bible, used by both churchgoers and non-churchgoers, is "Render unto Caesar the things that are Caesar's." We are going to look at that phrase, but it is important to note that it was followed by another one, and the rest of that statement is the main point of Jesus's command.

The Pharisees had a plot brewing; they wanted Jesus dead. So, they tried to trap Him with His own words. They thought if they could get Him to say the wrong thing, either against Rome or His fellowman, they could have Him arrested. But time after time, Jesus spoke just the right thing and evaded their trap.

In this instance, recorded in Matthew 22, the Pharisees enlisted the help of the Herodians. The Herodians were a political party loyal to Herod and, by extension, Rome. Though the Pharisees and the Herodians hated each other, they were putting their forces together to make sure Jesus was arrested. They came up with a plan and sent one of their own disciples to Jesus with this question, "Teacher, we know that you are true, and teach the way of God in truth; nor do you care about anyone, for you do not regard the person of men. Tell us, therefore, what do you think? Is it lawful to pay taxes to Caesar, or not?' (Matthew 22:16-17).

Can you hear the false sincerity? Do you see how they have caged Him in? If Jesus says it's against the law to pay taxes, then He is mounting an uprising against Rome. If He says it is the law, then He's defending Rome's oppressive abuse. I've got to admit, every time I read this, I can't help but think, wow, how's He going to get out of this? But Jesus perceived their intentions, requested a denarius, held it up and simply asked one question, "Whose image and inscription is this?" They answered with the only answer they could— "Caesar."

> **"And he said to them, 'Render therefore to Caesar the things that are Caesar's, and to God the things that are God's.' When they had heard these words, they marveled, and left him and went their way."** Matthew 22:21-22

They marveled. Their jaws dropped. To understand the full impact of Jesus's statement here, you have to think like a Jewish person and know the history of the Jewish people. What made them amazed, what made them marvel, was how Jesus turned this question around on His accusers while at the same time, without saying it out loud, called Caesar a fake, a counterfeit, and a false god.

When Jesus asked whose image and inscription was engraved, every Jewish person in that crowd connected these words to the ten commandments they knew by memory. Listen to the first two:

1. I am the Lord God; thou shalt have no other gods before Me.
2. Thou shalt not make unto thee any graven images.

Jesus had chosen His words carefully. That coin engraved in silver with the face of Caesar proclaiming "Caesar is god" was nothing less than idolatry.

Then He commanded the people to give that man what he requires, and give to God what He requires. I used to think the last part was a little tag on, as if Jesus was saying, "Render unto Caesar what is Caesar's and be good Jewish people." But the reality is the loaded part of the second half of this command. The Jewish people all knew from their Scriptures what God required, and Jesus was asking them, *have you given to God what He requires?*

Before we go on, in case you are asking, should I be paying taxes, listen to what Paul says in Romans 13:1-7: "Let everyone be subject to the governing authorities, for there is no authority except that which God has established. Consequently, whoever rebels against the authority is rebelling against what God has instituted, and those who do so will bring judgment on themselves. This is also why you pay taxes, for the authorities are God's servants, who give their full time to governing. Give to everyone what you owe them: If you owe taxes, pay taxes; if revenue, then revenue; if respect, then respect; if honor, then honor."

Yes, we should pay our taxes, but that's just the first half of this message. Don't miss that Jesus had something more significant to say. Give to God what God requires. Deuteronomy 10:12-13 helps us understand what God expects: "And now, Israel, what does the Lord your God ask of you but to fear the Lord your God, to walk in obedience to him, to love him, to serve the Lord your God with all your heart and with all your soul, and to observe the Lord's commands and decrees that I am giving you today for your own good."

Micah 6:8 says this, "He has shown you, O mortal, what is good. And what does the Lord require of you? To act justly and to love mercy and to walk humbly with your God." And Jesus, when asked about what God required, made it pretty simple. "Then they asked him, 'What must we do to do the works God requires?' Jesus answered, 'The work of God is this: to believe in the one he has sent'" (John 6:28-29).

What does God require of you? To believe in the One He has sent, to love Him, to obey Him, to serve Him with all of your heart, mind, and soul. That is so little in return for what He has done for us. So little when you think that He gave His Son to die on the cross to pay off our sin debt, fill us with His Spirit, and give us eternal life and the promise of Heaven forever. We owe Him everything.

Read: Psalms 116:12, Matthew 22:36-40, Luke 20:20-26, 1 Peter 2:13-17

Reflect: Am I giving God what He requires of me or am I holding back?

Pray: God, I owe You everything. I want to give You all of me, holding nothing back, fully surrendered.

CHAPTER 19

YOUR RIGHTEOUSNESS MUST EXCEED THAT OF THE PHARISEES

> *Our works do not generate righteousness, rather our righteousness in Christ generates works.* —Martin Luther

The Pharisees who were constantly trying to trap Jesus were powerful men. The common people feared these religious leaders because they had tremendous influence, unmatched Biblical knowledge, and an apparent connection straight to God. But these men were also lining their pockets through their religion and power, and I believe that people saw through it. I think the common people looked at the Pharisees and, in some way, wondered, is that real? Is their religion and all their carrying on legitimate?

Jesus couldn't have been more different from the religious elite and quickly gained influence and followers, with crowds following Him everywhere He went. Out of jealousy, the Pharisees and other religious leaders started to mix in the crowds, observing, asking hard questions, and causing dissension. As we've already seen, Jesus wasn't intimidated by or fearful of the Pharisees. He spoke to them directly with very hard truths and used their poor example to teach others how to follow God. Like in Matthew 5, during the Sermon on the Mount, when Jesus's teaching took a surprising turn:

> **"For I tell you that unless your righteousness surpasses that of the Pharisees and the teachers of the law, you will certainly not enter the Kingdom of Heaven."** Matthew 5:20

Was Jesus really saying that to enter the Kingdom of Heaven, one needs to be *more* righteous than these religious leaders who were held up as examples of righteousness? How could that even be possible?

Later, in Matthew 23, Jesus has more to say on this subject when He clearly condemns the Pharisees. Listen to His words in verse 13: "Woe to you, teachers of the law and Pharisees, you hypocrites! You shut the door of the Kingdom of Heaven in people's faces. You yourselves do not enter, nor will you let those enter who are trying to."

What an incredible thing to say to the most spiritual-looking people in all of Israel. By all appearances, no one could hold a candle to these men who exercised their religious tradition in a very public way. Dressed in their fine robes and linen with their tassels dangling off, they were known to draw attention to themselves in prayer and fasting so everyone could see how religious they really were. Yet, Jesus was saying they would not enter Heaven.

Jesus continues His condemnation of the Pharisees by comparing them to whitewashed tombs, beautiful on the outside but full of dead men's bones on the inside. They tithed but neglected the heart of God's law—justice, mercy, and faithfulness. These men acted religious on the outside, but there was something wrong, something insidious and evil going on inside. These religious leaders were hypocrites of the highest order. Frauds, by all accounts.

Remember the definition of hypocrite? People who dress up and act like someone else on stage. Now, it's important to remember that the actor never actually becomes the person they are portraying; they are just acting. They put on a costume and makeup, and they act like this person for as long as the production or movie lasts. But at the end of the day, the costume comes off, the makeup is washed away, and they return to the person they were before it started.

One theme that seems to repeat itself throughout Scripture is that becoming right and holy before God is an inside-out job, not an outside-in job. In Matthew 23:25, Jesus explains, "Woe to you teachers of the law and Pharisees, you hypocrites! You clean the outside of the cup and dish, but inside they are full of greed and self-indulgence. Blind Pharisee! First clean the inside of the cup and dish, and then the outside also will be clean."

Friends, when it comes to our faith, far too many of us are playing dress-up. We put on our Christian clothes and our Christian faces. We live out empty religious routines but never actually learn what it means to be a genuine follower of Christ. We have been sold a cheap grace that says that all you have to do to become a follower of Jesus is recite a sinner's prayer, feel bad for your sin for a few moments, and then maybe, if you feel like it, get baptized. Then you can move on with your life, your ticket to Heaven punched. Friends, that Gospel doesn't exist in the Bible. The true Good News of Jesus Christ is powerful. God sent His precious, innocent, sinless Son to die on the cross, a humiliating and excruciating death, and He expects much more from us than some flippant, half-committed response that creates no evident change in our lifestyle.

As we examine our lives, I (Stacey) would like to give you three sure-fire ways of not becoming like the Pharisees—all religious on the outside but dead on the inside.

STEP 1: KNOW JESUS.

It is incredibly ironic that these men knew every word of Scripture, yet when Jesus stood right in front of them, they completely missed it. They were filled with nothing more than religious information when what they desperately needed was spiritual transformation and revelation. You see, information lives in our minds, but transformation and revelation happen within our hearts. A genuine believer truly knows God, not just knows about Him.

How can you truly know Jesus? The answers are frustratingly simple. We have to spend time with Him, get on our knees in humble prayer, and speak to our Savior, the one who loves us. And we have to open the dusty book that sits on our bed stand or the app that remains unopened on our phones. We need to read the Bible, understand, and believe.

STEP 2: DO WHAT JESUS SAYS.

The Apostle John writes in I John 2:4, "If someone claims, 'I know God', but doesn't obey God's commandments, that person is a liar and is not living in the truth."

The Pharisees knew the Word of God, but they did not live it out in their everyday lives. They were famous for pushing rules and regulations on everybody else but completely avoiding them in their own lives. Jesus doesn't call us to simply recite a prayer and get baptized. He commands us to follow Him each and every day, obeying all that He has commanded us.

STEP 3: STOP SINNING.

Somewhere in this season of a seeker-friendly Gospel, the idea was born that you don't have to worry about addressing the sin in your life to be a Christian. Just attend church, sip lattes, and sing worship songs with tears and emotion, and then walk out of these doors and go back to whatever R-rated lifestyle you've been living. Continue in your sexual lives, your favorite TV series, or play filthy video games that are completely disconnected from the person of Christ.

Remember Paul's admonition in Philippians 2:12 to "continue to work out your salvation with fear and trembling." The day you accepted Jesus as Lord, you didn't cross a spiritual finish line; you stepped across the starting line. When you and I plunged down into the waters of baptism and raised up to a new life, we weren't handed a medal or a trophy. We were handed a cross.

In Luke 9:23, Jesus says these words about those who follow Him: "If anyone would come after me, let him deny himself and take up his cross daily and follow me." Jesus died for us, and we are called to pick up that cross that only meant death to anyone who picked it up. It's only in daily dying to ourselves and taking up the cross of Christ that we can truly find the righteousness that exceeds that of the Pharisees, the righteousness that leads to eternal life.

Read: Luke 11:46-54, John 8:39-47, John 14:15

Reflect: What area am I "playing dress-up"?

Pray: God, forgive me for the times when I do the "right things" on the outside, but don't allow You to transform my heart. Today, I choose to take up the cross and die to myself.

CHAPTER 20

BE PERFECT

For whoever keeps the whole law and yet stumbles at just one point is guilty of breaking all of it. —James, the brother of Jesus

In high school, I (Stacey) ran track and field. One year, I peaked at just the right time and was invited to participate in the high jump at the state championship. That morning, the officials called the athletes over and let us know where they would place the opening bar that day, five feet ten inches. You could hear a collective sigh of disbelief. Even though we had all jumped hundreds of times to get to this point, this new standard of success was higher. Very few athletes would clear the opening jump.

As I think back on that event, do you know what I don't remember? I don't remember the officials ever walking up to any of us as individual athletes and asking us, "Hey, where would you like us to start today? Stacey, what would make you comfortable this morning? Because we'd like to set the bar to a place that you feel good about." What did happen is those officials told us where the standard would be, they raised it to that point, and then they said, "If you can clear it, you can continue, and if you don't, you'll be disqualified."

In Matthew 5, Jesus sets the standard for success in the Christian life. In the last chapter, we saw Him demanding from us a righteousness greater than that of the Pharisees, but now He sets the bar even higher.

> **"Be perfect, therefore, as your heavenly Father is perfect."**
> **Matthew 5:48**

If you are like me, you might ask the question, I wonder what Jesus meant when He said perfect? Surely, in the translation from Greek to English, there was some confusion, and it doesn't really mean perfect. But if we look at Jesus's statement, we'll recognize that God is the standard.

He commands us to be perfect even as our Father in Heaven is perfect. Perfect means perfect in the purest sense of the word.

Now, it's important to note that this wasn't some new theology Jesus introduced. Throughout the Old Testament, God communicated the same expectation of perfection. Leviticus 19:2 demands, "Be holy because I, the Lord your God, am holy."

When the Jewish people received this instruction, they had a tangible reminder in their lives that God was supremely holy and pure. That reminder came in the form of a large curtain that hung in the temple, separating the people from the Holy of Holies, the place where the *shekinah* glory, the Spirit of God, dwelled in all His power and majesty. Because it was such a pure and powerful place, God warned that anyone who went behind the curtain would surely die.

Only once a year, the High Priest was allowed to pull back the corner of this curtain and step inside the Holy of Holies. Before this moment, he went through tremendous purification rites, sacrifices, and ritual washings. The whole community of Israel would gather outside and, in hushed silence, wondering if he would come back alive. As the High Priest entered, he would offer a sacrifice on behalf of all the people of Israel so they could find forgiveness for their sins.

That same holiness, that unapproachability of God, still exists today because His perfection and our brokenness remain unchanged. So, what do we do with Jesus's command for perfection? We know we are not perfect. As hard as we try to be good, as hard as we try to be like Christ, we continue to sin.

What do we do with this massive shortcoming? What are the consequences of not keeping God's command of perfection? Paul makes it clear in Romans 6:23 that "the wages of sin is death." This is not a promise of immediate physical death, but rather, it is a promise of eternal spiritual death and the torment of a real place called Hell.

I know there are many churches, pastors, blogs, and websites that claim there is no ultimate penalty for sin and that God will welcome all people into Heaven regardless of their choices and decisions. But friends, that is a lie. There is no more verifiable truth in Scripture than the reality of Hell and its terrible punishments. Just as sobering is the reality that all it takes to get there is simply one sin. One sin, one single moment of indiscretion severs our relationship with God and seals off our entry into Heaven for eternity.

For those that may have a fairly high opinion of themselves and believe that they are a good person, pay attention to the words of Paul in Romans 3:10-12: "There is no one righteous, not even one; there is no one who understands; there is no one who seeks God. All have turned away, they have together become worthless; there is no one who does good, not even one."

Standing before God the playing field is leveled. No one stands higher than another. Morally, we are all imperfect and guilty. So again, I ask, what are we supposed to do with this command to be perfect?

The answer to that question is the heart of the Gospel, the reason why Jesus took on human form. Hebrews explains, "For God's will was for us to be made holy by the sacrifice of the body of Jesus Christ, once for all time. Under the old covenant, the priest stands and ministers before the altar day after day, offering the same sacrifices again and again, which can never take away sins. But our High Priest Jesus, offered himself to God as a single sacrifice for sins, good for all time.... For by that one offering he forever made perfect those who are being made holy" (Hebrews 10:10-12, 14 NLT).

Incredible. These few verses are packed with so many truths. Let me highlight three:

1. GOD MADE A WAY.

God knew that you and I would sin and fall short of His perfection. He set the standard we could not meet, but He also made a way for us to "be made holy by the sacrifice of the body of Jesus Christ." The way to God is through the cross of Jesus Christ.

2. JESUS'S DEATH COVERS ALL SIN.

When Jesus died on the cross and His blood was shed on that wooden tree, He paid the penalty of our sins in full. That includes every sin we committed before we came to Christ and all the ways we fall short after we come to Him. There is not some angel in Heaven standing over a great eternal toggle switch that, every time you blow it, switches over to Hell, and when you repent, he flips it back to saved. You are covered under the grace and the love of Jesus Christ once, for all time.

3. GOD CAN MAKE IMPERFECT PEOPLE PERFECT.

Somehow, we are both perfect in God's eyes, but simultaneously, He is also making us holy. All you have to do is take a quick look at my life to know that I am not yet holy. Or ask my family. However, I have noticed that since I gave my heart to Jesus at age 22, there has been a process of change. I'm not the same man. The way I react to situations and the way I treat people is different. God has continued to do something in me—here's a big churchy word: sanctification. It's the process of holiness, becoming a little more like Jesus every day.

It is accurate to say that if you are a child of God, in an eternal sense, you are perfect. Your entrance into a heavenly home will be given because God sees you through the blood of Christ. But it's also true to say that in an earthly sense, you will continue to be refined, to be perfected, to be made holy in God's sight until you see Him face to face. We are perfect, yet being made holy.

Read: Philippians 3:12, Ephesians 3:12, Ephesians 5:1

Reflect: How do you feel about God's command to be perfect? What does it look like for you to be made holy today?

Pray: God, thank You for making a way for us to enter into Your presence. Without Jesus, I would never measure up, but through His sacrifice I am made perfect. Help me to learn to live a holy life.

CHAPTER 21

ENDURE PATIENTLY

Endurance is not just the ability to bear a hard thing, but to turn it into glory. —William Barclay

Human history is full of stories of endurance. One of those great stories is that of Sir Ernest Shackleton, who led three British expeditions to Antarctica in the early 1900s. In those days, there was no GPS or advanced technology, and Antarctica was as mysterious and remote as the back side of the moon. On one of his expeditions in 1915, disaster struck. The ship was trapped in ice and eventually sank. The crew survived by camping on the sea ice until it disintegrated, then by launching the lifeboats to reach a frigid and remote island. There was zero hope of rescue.

But Shackleton, intent on saving his men, launched on an impossible mission. Taking one lifeboat and two seasoned sailors, he set out from the island. Their dangerous and exhausting three-month journey over sea and land is one of the most eloquent examples in history of man's struggle to survive. Against all odds, they were able to secure ships and rescue the others. After two years in the icy wilderness, all twenty-seven men were saved. The British explorer Duncan Carse wrote about Shackleton's determination, "I do not know how they did it except they had to, three men of the heroic age with fifty feet of rope between them and a carpenter's ax." They endured.[20]

In the book of Revelation, Jesus gave messages to the early churches scattered around Asia. One of these seven churches was the church in Philadelphia. To that church, Jesus said,

> "I know your deeds. See I have placed before you an open door that no one can shut. I know that you have little strength, yet you have kept my Word and have not denied my name. Since you have kept my command to endure patiently, I will also keep you from the hour of trial that is going to come on the whole world to test the inhabitants of the earth. I'm coming soon. Hold on to what you have so no one will take your crown."
> Revelation 3:8, 10-11

Jesus was addressing the persecution happening to the early church and the persecution that would come. Persecution has visited the church its entire life and will continue as long as Satan rules this world. There are Christians today all over the world, being arrested, tortured, and brutally put to death. To these persecuted Christians, Jesus is saying, *Endure patiently.*

Endure, by definition, is *the capacity to hold out or bear up in the face of difficulty, with fortitude, steadfastness, and perseverance. To suffer patiently.*[21]

But what does this command to endure patiently mean for those of us who will likely never be arrested or tortured for our faith? There are many struggles in the Christian life—hard, bone-jarring, gut-wrenching, heart-breaking trials and tribulations. We all have stories of loss, abandonment, loneliness, sickness, and all kinds of temptation. If you're like me (Todd), these struggles can give way to this question: *God, why are you letting this happen to me?* We wonder if God loves us, why doesn't He stop the pain? Why doesn't He answer our prayers?

I have to tell you, when I first read this command, I got it wrong. It sounded to me a little like Jesus was saying, *trouble is coming; live with it. I command you to endure with a smile on your face, like it or not!* But that is not it at all. The words here are like a commander, leading men into battle. Jesus is saying, *Stand your ground, hold firm, don't give an inch, don't give up. Help is on the way. I know you have little strength, but there is a doorway, a window opened to Heaven, and I'm going to bring you through it. I'm coming back to rescue you and bring you home.*

In Hebrews 12, trials and suffering are referred to as God's discipline. Like a good father, God disciplines us out of love. As children, I doubt that any of us appreciated the discipline of our parents at the time. But looking back, we can see things differently. We understand that boundaries, rules, and discipline were not only necessary but were for our good.

God allows struggles in our lives to sculpt us into the image of His Son. Think of an artist with a chisel and a hammer creating a masterpiece. Every cut is painful, every hammer blow is bone-jarring, and we might not understand in the moment what's happening to us or why, but eternity will show that God was sculpting us, shaping us, honing us, and seasoning us through trials.

In Hebrews 11, right before all the talk about discipline, we find a list of the champions of the faith. After celebrating many heroes from Jewish history, the writer explains there isn't enough time to tell of all the victories of those

> ...who through faith conquered kingdoms, administered justice, and gained what was promised; who shut the mouths of lions, quenched the fury of the flames, and escaped the edge of the sword; whose weakness was turned to strength; and who became powerful in battle and routed foreign armies. Women received back their dead, raised to life again, but there were others who were tortured, refusing to be released so that they might gain an even better resurrection. Some faced jeers and flogging and even chains and imprisonment. They were put to death by stoning, they were sawed in two; they were killed by the sword. They went about in sheepskins and goatskins, destitute, persecuted and mistreated, the world was not worthy of them. (Hebrews 11:33-38)

Did you notice the shift? "But there were others . . ." There were great champions who conquered armies and even raised the dead *and those* who were stoned and killed by the sword. Some champions won the battle, and others endured great persecution and torture. Like these men and women, many of you have endured with great patience and spiritual integrity everything that life has thrown at you, and you are here, and you remain.

Our greatest example of endurance comes from Jesus. Listen to Hebrews 12:1-2: "Let us run with perseverance the race marked out for us, fixing our eyes on Jesus, the pioneer and perfecter of faith. For the joy set before him he endured the cross, scorning its shame, and sat down at the right hand of the throne of God. Consider him who endured such opposition from sinners, so that you will not grow weary and lose heart."

What possible joyous thing in the future helped Jesus endure six hours of agony on the cross? You and me! The joy that helped Jesus endure through clenched teeth and cries of pain was the reality that we would be saved! When we face challenges, we need to consider Him, who endured so much for us, so we don't lose heart and give up.

Paul compared the Christian life to running a marathon. "I have fought the good fight, I have finished the race, I have kept the faith. Now there is in store for me the crown of righteousness, which the Lord the righteous Judge will award to me on that day – and not only to me, but also to all who have longed for his appearing" (II Timothy 4:7-8).

For years, I had a picture hanging in my office—a full page from USA Today with a man's picture and byline, advertising the coming summer Olympics. The man, John Stephen Akhwari, was a marathon runner in the 1968 Olympic Games in Mexico City, representing Tanzania. During the race, Akhwari cramped up due to the high altitude of the city he wasn't used to. At the 19-kilometer point of a 42-kilometer race, there was a jockeying for position; he fell, dislocating his knee and injuring his shoulder. Of the 75 competitors who started the race, Akhwari was one of only 57 who completed the race. Over an hour after the first competitor had crossed the finish line, with only a few thousand people left in the stadium, Akhwari hobbled across the line. When asked later why he continued running, he said, "My country did not send me 5,000 miles to start the race; they sent me 5,000 miles to finish the race." And he did.[22]

Earnest Shackleford's ship, christened to make the arduous journey to Antarctica was called the *Endurance.* To find a crew Earnest Shackleton reportedly placed an advertisement in *The Times,* reading: "Men wanted for hazardous journey. Small wages, bitter cold, long months of complete darkness, constant danger, safe return doubtful. Honor and recognition in case of success."[23]

We are called to endure. Rescue is coming. Whatever your particular struggle is, whatever life throws at you along the way, you are called to finish the race. If you are struggling, if you are asking why, if you don't know how things will end, or if they will end, fix your eyes on Jesus. One day, all of the challenges of life will appear in eternity like a single drop in a vast ocean of God's grace and His reward. Hold on!

Endure Patiently

Read: Romans 15:5-6, 1 Thessalonians 1:3, Hebrews 12:5-11

Reflect: Are you enduring patiently? Or are you growing weary?

Pray: Jesus, I look to You and Your example of endurance. Please give me strength and focus to endure and remain strong.

SECTION 4

RELATIONSHIPS

By this everyone will know that you are my disciples,
if you love one another.

John 13:35

CHAPTER 22

BECOME A SERVANT

What work does Christ set his servants to do? The way that they serve him, he tells them, is by becoming the slaves of their fellow servants and being willing to do literally anything, however costly, irksome, or undignified, in order to help them. This is what love means, as he himself showed at the last supper when he played the slave's part and washed the disciples' feet. —James Packer

The disciples James and John were known for their quick tempers, earning them the nickname Sons of Thunder. On one occasion, when they traveled with Jesus to Samaria and the Samaritans refused to supply food and lodging, James and John were enraged and asked Jesus to kill those Samaritans, reigning down fire and brimstone. On another occasion, the bold and arrogant brothers asked Jesus if they could rule with Him for all eternity, sitting on His right and left hand.

As you can imagine, this presumptuous request didn't sit well with the other ten disciples. As tensions rose, Jesus called them all together. He quickly reminded them that His kingdom differed from the Gentile rulers who lorded their authority over others. Greatness in the kingdom of God was to be defined by servanthood.

> "Not so with you. Instead, whoever wants to become great among you must be your servant, and whoever wants to be first must be slave of all. For even the Son of Man did not come to be served, but to serve, and to give his life as a ransom for many." Mark 10:43-45

Jesus had a radical message for the hotheaded disciples—if you want to become great, forget about being on the right and left of the throne; instead, be a servant. The word for servant here is *doulos*, translated as *slave to all*. This concept and Greek word appear more than 120 times throughout the New Testament.

For Americans, the word *slave* is associated with the dark days when African Americans were kept enslaved for life against their will in squalid situations with chains, manacles, and whips—where there was no way out but fleeing or death. The New Testament term presents a different concept: the indentured servant. An indentured servant was typically a poor person who presented himself to a wealthy person for a life of service in exchange for provision. A contract was drawn up, and the wealthy would agree to let this man, and often his wife and children, come into the home or property and work for them until he was back on his feet.

The precedent for this type of arrangement is found in the Old Testament. God told Moses in the law that a poor Hebrew could become a bondservant for an agreed-upon time that could not exceed seven years. In the seventh year, the servant was set free, but God gave a provision: "But if your servant says to you, 'I do not want to leave you,' because he loves you and your family and is well off with you, then take an awl and push it through his earlobe into the door, and he will become your servant for life. Do the same for your female servant" (Deuteronomy 15:16-17).

Notice the condition: *He loves you and your family and is well off.* The man became an indentured servant or *doulos* when, out of love, he willingly chose to become a servant for life. This Old Testament relationship is a picture of our relationship with Christ, surrendering as bondservants, indentured for life.

In the 1850s, an Englishman, who made his fortune mining in the California gold rush, was returning to England. On the way, he stopped in New Orleans. One day while walking through the town, he came to the slave market. He observed men bidding with great interest on a beautiful black woman. Their demeanor and lewd comments left no question of their evil intentions toward her. His heart revolted against the whole mess.

As the bids rose, the Englishman offered twice the last bid, much higher than had ever been paid for a slave in New Orleans, and the sale was made. The man went to the block to claim the woman he had purchased. As she came down one step and stood just about eye level with him, she spat in his face and hissed at him through clenched teeth, "I hate you." He wiped the spit away and said nothing. He then took her by the hand and led her to an office building.

The Englishman went to the desk and made a request. The man at the desk started to protest, but the Englishman insisted, "You must do it; it's the law." Finally, a transaction was completed, and the Englishman gave the woman, who was still fuming like a beast, the paper with an official seal. The man informed her, "These are your freedom papers; you're free."

Not understanding, she hissed at him again, "I hate you."

"But don't you understand? Here are your papers, you're free," the man said.

"No," she said, bewildered, "I don't understand; you paid twice as much for me as any other buyer in New Orleans, and now you are giving me my freedom? I don't believe you; I can't believe you."

"Yes, these are your papers, signed, sealed." And he put them in her hand.

"Do you mean," she said, "That you bought me to set me free?"

"Yes, that is why I bought you, to set you free," the man said.

Then tears came up into her eyes, her face softened, and she slipped to her knees, reaching down she put her hands on those rough miner's boots, laid her cheek on the toe of one of them, and through her tears said, "You bought me to set me free, you bought me to set me free?" And choking through her tears, she looked up at the man and said, "Sir, all I want in life is to be your slave because you bought me to set me free."[24]

Let me (Todd) remind you that before you were a Christian, you were a slave to sin. Not just a bondservant, but enslaved, entrapped, forever in the chains of sin and death. And Christ rescued you. Through His death on the cross, He purchased you and set you free. Now Christ is calling to us, *I've set you free from sin and death; would you, in return, become my bondservant? Because of My great love for you, would you, in return, become a bondservant to all?*

We're meant to be in a relationship with one another more than just fellowship suppers or small groups, more than just saying, "I'll pray about that for you." We should live with each other in such a loving, intimate way that we feel we are, in fact, indebted to each other and have committed our life and love to each other. Pierced ears, all of us, slaves to Christ and slaves to each other.

Paul summarizes it well in Philippians 2:5-8: "In your relationships with one another, have the same mindset as Christ Jesus: Who, being in very nature God, did not consider equality with God something to be used to his own advantage; rather, he made himself nothing by taking the very nature of a servant, being made in human likeness. And being found in appearance as a man, he humbled himself by becoming obedient to death—even death on a cross!"

Just imagine what the church could look like if our attitude toward one another was that of a bondservant: How can I serve you? What if we treated our parents, our spouse, our children, our church family, and our community this way?

Greatness in God's kingdom is found when we serve one another.

Read: John 13:4-17, Ephesians 6:5-9, Romans 6:17-18, 1 Peter 2:16

Reflect: How well am I serving others?

Pray: God, help me to be great in Your kingdom. First, by serving You with my whole life. And second, by loving and serving others.

CHAPTER 23

WHAT GOD HAS JOINED TOGETHER, LET NO MAN SEPARATE

Sex is not an evil curse we have to curb and deny. It's a good gift we get to enjoy, as long as it's in the right context. —John Mark Comer

There's one moment in every wedding that, as the pastor, I (Stacey) love because I have a unique perspective. It's that point when the song changes, the doors open, and the groom sees his bride for the first time in her beautiful wedding dress. I make it a point to watch him because there's something so powerful about the recognition and beauty of that moment. You see the appreciation and love as she walks closer, and she finally looks up and meets his eye. It's such an amazing thing to see their love brought together.

Outside of our decision to follow Jesus, the decision to be wed and united into one is the most important and profound relationship decision we will ever make, for better or for worse. In Mark 10, Jesus addresses this very topic. We find Him in another one of those sticky conversations with the Pharisees when they attempt to trap Him by asking, "Should a man be allowed to divorce his wife?"

As Jesus was known to do, He responded to their question with one of His own: "What did Moses say in the law about divorce?" The Pharisees responded that Moses said a man could give his wife a certificate of divorce and send her away. But that was a half-truth. What Moses actually said was, "If a man marries a woman, but she becomes displeasing to him because he finds some indecency in her, he may write her a certificate of divorce" (Deuteronomy 24:1 BSB). This isn't an open license to divorce a spouse for any reason. There needed to be some indecency found in the marriage. But as man's sinful heart tends to do, the Pharisees took this idea of indecency and spun it into their own definition.

When Jesus responded, He didn't address their misuse of God's intended law. Instead, He pointed to a deeper truth spoken by God Himself.

> **"'It was because your hearts were hard that Moses wrote you this law,' Jesus replied. 'But at the beginning of creation God made them male and female. For this reason, a man will leave his father and mother and be united to his wife, and the two will become one flesh. So they are no longer two, but one flesh. Therefore, what God has joined together, let no one separate.'"** Mark 10:5-9

Notice in that last sentence who is doing the joining and bringing these people together in marriage—it is God Himself. Marriage was God's invention, His gift to humanity. You and I can decide to get married, we can get down on one knee and propose, and we can set a date for a wedding; but only God joins people together. As a result, when we decide to enter God's created institution of marriage, we should abide by His stated guidelines and boundaries.

It's important to remember that when God brought the first man and woman together in the garden, there was no ceremony, preacher, or exchanging of rings or vows. God used the supernatural act of sexual union to bring two people together in one powerful, emotional, and physically binding act—one that joins an individual man and an individual woman into one profound, supernatural being.

When God says what He has joined together, let no one separate, it reads as much as a warning as a command. Since the moment in the garden that God gave humanity the beautiful gift of intimacy and sexuality, we have tried to pluck it from its intended place, to use and misuse it in all kinds of places outside of the boundaries that God has set.

When Jesus said that the two would become one flesh, He meant it both as a spiritual fact and as a physical reality. This powerful, spiritual, emotional bond is created as much on a one-night stand as on a wedding night. Just because sexuality is being misused in our culture doesn't mean it's lost its binding supernatural power.

For some years, I worked at a family cabinet shop. To build a cabinet, you take pieces of wood, shape them, and glue them together. The places where the boards are glued together inevitably become the strongest joints in the cabinet. Occasionally we would make a mistake in construction and need to undo what has been glued together. Do you know what happens when you pull apart wood that has been properly glued? A mess. Shards of wood, pieces of each board left attached and glued to the other. Each piece of itself stuck to the other.

Within the confines of the intended purpose of the binding nature of sex, it is beautiful and wonderful, but when taken outside of God's design, its soul-combining properties become twisted and sinful. Just like you cannot pull apart glued cabinets without damage, there is a permanent binding when a man and woman engage in sex of any kind. Despite what our culture says, there is no such thing as casual sex. The Apostle Paul explains this in I Corinthians 6:16: "Do you not know that he who unites himself with a prostitute is one with her in body? For it is said, 'The two will become one flesh.'"

The result of cheapening and devaluing intimacy into some fun activity has created a generation of people who carry the emotional and spiritual remnants of an untold number of partners as they move from one encounter to another. Young people wonder why breaking up can be so devastating, crushing, and, many times, leading to feelings of suicide. It is because we have been lied to about sex. It is not just part of growing up, and contraception does not protect you from what sex does to your heart and your soul.

Today, many are deciding to move in together and skip marriage altogether. After all, if we never glue the wood together to begin with, it shouldn't be that difficult to pull it apart, right? However, that is a complete misunderstanding of the power of sex in God's created purpose for it. Remember, God's institution of marriage is consummated, perfected, and completed in the marriage bed. You may have skipped the paperwork and the wedding ceremony, but when you move in and hook up, you are still deciding to be "glued," connected permanently in body and spirit.

So, you might be asking, are you saying that we are married to all the people we have slept with? The answer as I read the Bible is "yes" and "no." "Yes," when two people have sex, they become one. But "no," you're not married legally in the law of the land. And "no," God does not consider living together a legitimate marriage either. When you cohabitate with someone, you're only living in sin, or what the Bible calls *fornication*. Anytime we have sex outside of marriage, we are living in complete opposition to God.

Let's switch gears and look at the second half of Jesus's words: "Let no one separate." The disciples were confused by Jesus's seemingly harsh words. Mark 10 tells us that later, when they were alone with Jesus, they started to ask questions.

Jesus responded to their questions: "Anyone who divorces his wife and marries another woman commits adultery against her. And if she divorces her husband and marries another man, she commits adultery" (Mark 10:11-12). It's hard to get our minds around the unvarnished simplicity and difficulty of Jesus's words here, especially in a society where we try to create loopholes and workarounds against any guardrail we find.

While it may feel uncaring and callous for Jesus to make such a blanket statement about divorce, His statement is more clearly a reflection of just how powerful the act of marriage is. Once a marriage has been legally and biblically formed, who should separate it? *No one.* God intends for marriage to be for keeps.

In Malachi 2:16 NLT, God makes a powerful statement: "'For I hate divorce!' says the LORD, the God of Israel. 'To divorce your wife is to overwhelm her with cruelty,' says the LORD of Heaven's Armies. 'So, guard your heart; do not be unfaithful to your wife.'" We have all seen how divorce can break down the family. It is one of the most painful things any human will ever endure.

The Bible has given us two clear situations when divorce is permitted but not mandated. These are an extramarital affair or abandonment by a non-Christian or unbelieving spouse. Jesus states in Matthew 5:32: "But I tell you that anyone who divorces his wife, except for sexual immorality, makes her the victim of adultery, and anyone who marries a divorced woman commits adultery." And the Apostle Paul says in I Corinthians 7:15 NLT, "But if the husband or wife who isn't a believer insists on leaving, let them go. In such cases the believing husband or wife is no longer bound to the other, for God has called you to live in peace."

I'd like to recognize that it leaves questions about situations involving serious issues, like abuse. If you are in an abusive situation, it is critical that you find help and get to a place of safety.

But friends, as I look back over my years of ministry and counseling people, adultery, abuse, and unbelieving spouses are not the only three reasons people are leaving marriages. Like the Jewish people in Jesus's time, we have found all kinds of reasons to dissolve a union that God intended to be forever.

But as followers of Jesus, we are called to be different. We are supposed to love our spouses as Jesus loves us. Do you remember the condition you were in when Jesus found you? When you had nothing to offer Him but guilt, brokenness, and shame? And He looked at us in our helpless condition and said, "Father, forgive him, for he does not know what he's doing."

Romans 8:38-39 describes God's love: "For I am convinced that neither death nor life, neither angels nor demons, neither the present nor the future, nor any powers, neither height nor depth, nor anything else in all creation, will be able to separate us from the love of God that is in Christ Jesus our Lord."

That's how much we have been loved. And that grace, that kind of love, is what we've been called to give to our spouse in our marriage.

Read: Genesis 2:18-25, I Corinthians 6:18-20, Hebrews 13:4

Reflect: What is my view of marriage? Do I have the same honor and respect for it that Jesus did?

Pray: God, thank You for the gift of marriage. Help me to have the same honor, love, and respect for marriage You do.

CHAPTER 24

HONOR YOUR PARENTS

The origin of society and the family is sustained only as the authority and the rule of the heads [parents] of the house are upheld and respected. The command, then, to honor parents may be justly regarded as asserting the foundation of all social ordinances and arrangements. Where parents are not honored, a flaw lies at the basis and the stability of the entire social fabric is endangered.
—*The Pulpit Commentary*

When God gave the Ten Commandments, six dealt specifically with how we're to treat the people in our lives, and five of those six are "do not" commands: Do not steal, do not kill, etc. Only one of those six commandments is something that we are commanded to *do*. "Honor your father and your mother, as the Lord your God has commanded you, so that you may live long and that it may go well with you in the land of the Lord your God is giving you" (Deuteronomy 5:15).

I don't know about your experience, but I (Stacey) have found that honoring my parents has become easier as I've become a parent myself. Being a parent has both amazing times and challenging times. In those challenging times, it's hard not to think back to the tremendous hardship that I put my parents through and appreciate them even more.

I lost my dad when I was young, but my mom has always been wonderful. Like many of you, if I managed to do anything positive in my teenage years, it was to improve my mom's prayer life greatly. I can still remember the worst thing my mom ever called me, during a moment of complete exasperation, which I rightfully earned when she looked at me with words so powerful that it sent chills down the spine of everyone in our house, "You nincompoop."

For a long time, I thought this was a word my mom had made up just for me, but I found out it has a definition. *Nincompoop: a stupid or silly person, a fool, or a simpleton.*[25] Mom, if you're reading this, I'd like to publicly admit that you were right. I can say with confidence that I was a terrible teenager, and honoring my mother was the farthest thing from my little self-centered universe.

From the beginning of time, we have seen children disobeying their parents and causing problems. The Bible doesn't hide the flaws of its people and gives us many examples. Of the first two siblings, Cain killed Abel; then we find Noah's son, Ham, was so wicked in the way that he lived that God rejected his entire generation. Isaac's son Jacob would deceive his father and steal the birthright from his older brother. David's sons humiliated him in public. Lot's daughters took terrible advantage of their dad.

When you find children in the Bible, it's not uncommon to find discord, dishonor, and disobedience toward their parents. Jesus addressed this issue in Matthew 15 by quoting directly from the Ten Commandments:

> **"And why do you, by your traditions, violate the direct commandments of God? For instance, God says, 'Honor your father and mother and anyone who speaks disrespectfully of their father or mother must be put to death.' But you say it is all right for people to say to their parents, 'Sorry, I can't help you. For I have vowed to give to God what I would have given to you.'"** Matthew 15:3-5

Surprisingly, Jesus wasn't speaking to children when He gave this command. He was talking to a group of adults, the religious leaders. The context for this discussion came when these lawmakers created a way for children to commit all their money and future earnings to the temple. This commitment, or *corban*, didn't have to be given immediately. Many adult children were saying they would give their money to God in the future while secretly spending it on their own comforts while their elderly parents lived in poverty and need. Once again, the people of Israel valued religious practice over God's principles.

Let's take a minute to examine this simple command to honor our parents and discover some important truths tucked into its words.

TRUTH #1: THERE ARE NO CONDITIONS CONNECTED TO THIS COMMAND.

I want to highlight that Jesus's command does not have an age limit. It's easy to pigeonhole this command to honor your parents to children or teenagers, but it is binding for life. It's no exaggeration that you and I are commanded to show honor to our parents every day of our lives.

There is also no condition on the quality of the parenting. Understandably, when some of you hear this command, your first thought is, *but you don't know my parents*. There is no denying that some of you have had dreadful mothers and fathers. Every day, people conceive children without intent or desire to raise them. Of all the great responsibility and honors that this life bestows upon us, I can't think of another one that comes as easy and too often to completely unqualified people as becoming a parent does.

If you have had parents who have acted in painful indifference or even abuse toward you, the Lord recognizes your pain, He recognizes your parents' shortcomings and sins, and He does not excuse them. But the same Jesus who commanded us to love our enemies and pray for those who persecute us has also commanded us to honor our fathers and mothers. God gave the command, and Jesus confirmed it without one "if, but, or" condition— only honor.

TRUTH #2: FOLLOWING THIS COMMAND PROMISES A SIGNIFICANT BLESSING.

The Apostle Paul reminds us of this promise: "Children, obey your parents in the Lord, for this is right. 'Honor your father and mother'— which is the first commandment with a promise— 'so that it may go well with you and that you may enjoy long life on the earth'" (Ephesians 6:1-3).

Notice that this promise is for the here and now. Your Heavenly Father is giving you His word that your life here on earth today can be filled with health and vitality if you obey His command to treat your parents with honor and respect. Think about that. Of all the things we do to improve our lives—going to the gym, dieting, listening to podcasts, investing money well, and working with life coaches— what if the best thing we could do to improve our lives right now is to honor our father and mother? If we know God is poised and ready to pour out a spiritual blessing on us from His eternal resources, why not begin today?

TRUTH #3: NOT FOLLOWING THIS COMMAND WILL BRING THE OPPOSITE OF A BLESSING.

What if one of the reasons that things in your life seem to go wrong and that you can never seem to get ahead or stay healthy is directly connected to the dishonor and disdain you show for your parents? God had sobering words in Deuteronomy 21 to the parents of stubborn and rebellious children. They are told to bring the child who won't obey to the town elders. Then, the men of the town are commanded to stone him to death.

While we no longer are under the strict Old Testament law, I Timothy 5:8 NLT tells us: "Those who won't care for their relatives, especially those in their own household, have denied the true faith. Such people are worse than unbelievers." It's also interesting that one of the signs of the return of Jesus Christ is the unraveling of the family. Listen to 2 Timothy 3:1-2: "But mark this: There will be terrible times in the last days. People will be lovers of themselves, lovers of money, boastful, proud, abusive, disobedient to their parents, ungrateful, unholy." Did you note how disobedience to parents is a sign of the last days? It is against this rebellion that the Spirit of God will one day return and judge the entire earth.

The good news is that it's not too late. Today, we have the opportunity to obey Jesus's command. We can repent, seek God's forgiveness, and begin showing honor from this day forward.

Jesus Himself is our best example of a son who honored His Father. This respect is evident throughout the Gospels, but especially in Jesus's sacrifice for us. Philippians 2:8 speaks of Jesus's obedience, "And being found in appearance as a man, he humbled himself by becoming obedient to death—even death on a cross!"

Read: Proverbs 23:22, Matthew 26:36-42, Philippians 2:5-8

Reflect: What does it look like for me to honor my parents today?

Pray: Jesus, thank You for Your example of a child honoring their Father. Help me to love, honor, and respect my parents.

CHAPTER 25

LOVE YOUR NEIGHBOR AS YOURSELF

To love my neighbor as myself [means] something unbelievably powerful and earthshaking and reconstructing and overturning and upending will have to happen in our souls. Something supernatural. Something well beyond what self-preserving, self-enhancing, self-exalting, self-esteeming, self-advancing human beings like John Piper can do on their own.   —John Piper

I (Stacey) recently read an article by the Heritage Foundation. According to their best estimation, there are about 4,500 United States federal laws that define over 300,000 federal crimes. In an attempt to stem the tide of a society falling apart, we try to legislate morality. But have you noticed despite the increasing number of laws and regulations, violence and lawlessness continue to rise?[26]

Jesus was no stranger to legalism that attempted transformation. The litigious religious leaders, who thrived in adding rules and regulations but failed to apply those rules to themselves, approached Jesus with the question of all questions—what is the greatest commandment in the Law of Moses? Jesus took all the Law and summarized it this way:

> **"Jesus replied: 'Love the Lord your God with all your heart and with all your soul and with all your mind. This is the first and greatest commandment. And the second is like it: Love your neighbor as yourself. All the Law and the Prophets hang on these two commandments.'"**   Matthew 22:37-40

We have already looked at the command to love God in chapter six. Now, we are going to dive into the command, "Love your neighbor as yourself." These five words of Jesus are revolutionary. While society claims that our value comes from where we were born, our gender, our birth order, our family, or our social standing, Jesus is telling us that all human beings have equal value. Everyone should love their neighbors because every person was created in God's image with intrinsic value from the moment they are conceived. Obeying this command and placing value on human life has brought about the abolition of slavery, the creation of hospitals, orphanages, universities, and aid organizations like the Red Cross, Samaritan's Purse, the Salvation Army, and countless others.

As we explore these powerful words, I'd like to ask some hard questions I have struggled to answer. I believe our ability to answer these questions is key to effectively carrying out Jesus's command to love our neighbor as ourselves.

Question 1: How does this command to love your neighbor as yourself fulfill and satisfy so many other commands?

I can remember reading these words of Jesus as a new believer and thinking, *wait, if I do these two things, you're telling me that all the rest of these thousands of words and commands in the Bible are somehow fulfilled?* As I wrestled with this question, God presented me with the Ten Commandments as a pattern. When you love God completely, the first four commands are automatically met: Have no other gods before me, don't bow down to idols, don't use the Lord's name in vain, and observe the Sabbath as unto the Lord. The next six commands after that are rooted in our need to love people. If I love the people around me, I won't murder them, steal from them, lie to them, commit adultery, or covet their things, and I most certainly will honor my mother and father.

Looking throughout the Bible, we see this same pattern repeatedly. All requirements of Scripture are met by loving God and loving people. Jesus was not only simplifying the complex system of Jewish law and tradition, but He was also simplifying our lives today. If you are wondering how you can find the purpose and the peace that you desire, I believe God would say to you, do two things: love Me with all your heart, soul, and mind; and love your neighbor as yourself.

Question 2: If Jesus is calling me to love my neighbor, then who is my neighbor? Who are these people that I'm supposed to lavish this care and compassion upon?

Conveniently, Jesus was asked the very same question. In Luke 10, He tells the story of a Jewish man traveling from Jerusalem to Jericho who was attacked by bandits and left for dead on the side of the road. A Jewish priest in all his garments and grandeur walked by, switched to the other side of the road, and continued. Then, a temple worker came by, saw the man's need, but left him in dire condition.

Then something unusual happened. A Samaritan, someone despised by the Jews, came by and felt compassion for the man. He soothed and bandaged his wounds, took him to an inn, and cared for him. The Samaritan then paid the bill upfront for the man's extended stay. As Jesus concluded the story, He looked at the crowd and asked, "'Which of these three do you think was a neighbor to the man who fell into the hands of robbers?' The expert in the law replied, 'The one who had mercy on him.' Jesus told him, 'Go and do likewise'" (Luke 10:36-37).

The Samaritan man who stopped to help the beaten Jewish man was no acquaintance or friend; they didn't live next door to each other. The only qualifier that Jesus gives to the battered man is that he was Jewish and he needed help. If we use this parable as our pattern to determine who our neighbor is, then any person at any time who is in need qualifies as our neighbor.

So, if we are supposed to follow the command to love our neighbor as ourselves, then we need to ask:

Question 3: How much do I love myself?

I'm ashamed to admit that, apparently, I like me a lot. I don't want to be self-centered. I sincerely try to be selfless and humble, but when I take an honest inventory of how much time I try to please myself on any given day, it's significant. I spend most of my day thinking about how I'm feeling and how I might make myself feel even better. If I get a little hungry, I try to find food I love to eat. If I need a little exercise, I skip it. If someone makes me uncomfortable, that's okay; I insulate myself from them and find people who make me happy.

The Apostle Paul says it best in Ephesians 5:29: "After all, no one ever hated their own body, but they feed and care for their body." If I'm going to love other people like I love myself, it means I have to begin thinking about and caring for others a lot because I care about me a lot!

Question 4: But what if I don't love myself?

There's a distinct possibility that someone reading this is thinking, *But I don't really love myself that much. In fact, some days, I don't feel like I like myself at all. How do I care for others if I don't care for myself?* These feelings are serious. There may be some legitimate issues going on in your life that have been a part of your past story that is impacting how you see the person in the mirror. I hope you'll take some time to go to your pastor or find a local Christian counselor and begin working through the foundation of those feelings and why they are there.

But with that said, Jesus solved even this complex question when He upgraded this command. Listen as He speaks in John 13:34: "So now I am giving you a new commandment: Love each other. Just as I have loved you, you should love each other." Trying to figure out how much I love me can get complicated, so instead of leaving the comparison of how I should care about others to my confused mind, Jesus gives the perfect example of what it means to love—Himself. With this standard, all excuses fly out the window. Whether you love yourself a lot or struggle to love yourself at all, the command is the same: love like Jesus.

Finally, one last question. This is the one that stops me in my tracks as I read this command. It's the part I struggle with the most:

Question 5: How can a person like me ever love like Jesus?

Knowing Christ and how He loved, how can I ever match up? How is it even possible to love like that with the heart that I have?

There is good news. Listen to the words of I John 4:16 NLT: "God is love, and all who live in love live in God, and God lives in them. And as we live in God, our love grows more perfect." Loving like Jesus is only possible through Jesus. The love you had when you became a Christian is not the love you should have five years later. Somehow, in some supernatural way, the love of God is perfected in us, and our ability to love the people around us like we've been called to do becomes more and more possible.

What you and I lack in our humanness, God provides in His power. He asks us to do hard things and then He provides us everything we need to do it. We only have to take Him up on His offer.

Love Your Neighbor As Yourself

Read: John 4:16-17, John 15:12-13, 1 John 2:7-11

Reflect: How well am I loving my neighbors?

Pray: God, thank You for Your perfect love. Help me see people with Your love and compassion. Show me how to share Your love today.

CHAPTER 26

DO UNTO OTHERS

Those who are not looking for happiness are the most likely to find it, because those who are searching forget that the surest way to be happy is to seek happiness for others. —Martin Luther King, Jr.

Turn from all known sin and spend your time in doing good. Try to live in peace with everyone; work hard at it.
—*Psalm 34:14 Living Bible*

When Jesus commanded us to love one another, He was talking about much more than a feeling. He was instructing us to love in word and deed. Jesus wants us to practice "love in action!" Thankfully, He gave us practical, tangible ways to do that. Even people unfamiliar with the Bible are probably familiar with the command commonly called "The Golden Rule." Like the two great commandments from Matthew 22, according to Jesus, this Golden Rule sums up all the Law in just a few short words.

> **"So, in everything, do to others what you would have them do to you, for this sums up the Law and the Prophets.**
> **Matthew 7:12**

Some have jokingly suggested that the Golden Rule means, whoever's got the gold rules! But it's really the very opposite of that. Jesus's command to "do unto others" describes a kind of love that is thoughtful, intentional, and sacrificial. "Golden" because this kind of love is the richest, the purest, the very best, and royal. If there is a love that wins a gold medal, it's this! Jesus said this one rule sums up what most of the Old Testament (the Law and the Prophets) had been exemplifying to the Jewish people.

If you have ever wondered what true love looks like, here is your answer. We know how to love best by simply asking ourselves how we would want someone else to love us. It means giving what we would like to receive.

In Luke 6:31, Luke records this same command: "Do to others as you would have them do to you." Right before those words, Jesus provides several practical examples. "Doing unto others" means loving your enemies and doing good to those who hate you. It means when someone tries to take something from you, you choose to give it willingly, or when someone slaps you on the cheek, you turn to them the other cheek.

Jesus is teaching us to show love by doing, even when we don't *feel* love.

Unfortunately, most people would define the Golden Rule as a love that is reactive. In other words, if someone slaps you, don't slap back. If someone steals from you, don't steal back. If someone hates you in various ways, don't hate back by hurting them like you've been hurt. Certainly, the way we react in those scenarios is part of the Golden Rule, but what if there's even more? What if Jesus means for us to be proactive in doing unto others?

Jesus didn't wait to show His love in a reactive way. He exemplified the Golden Rule by doing for others first. Listen to how Peter describes Jesus to the household of Cornelius: "You know what has happened throughout the province of Judea, beginning in Galilee after the baptism that John preached— how God anointed Jesus of Nazareth with the Holy Spirit and power, and how he went around doing good and healing all who were under the power of the devil, because God was with him" (Acts 10:37-38). The anointed, Spirit-filled Jesus got up every morning looking for ways to do good to others. Peter implies to Cornelius that Jesus's reputation for doing good had preceded Him and defined Him to all those living in Judea.

Let me suggest that practicing the Golden Rule–doing for others as you would have them do for you—is getting out in front of love. Don't wait for your love to be tested by your neighbors when they hurt you. Do good to them now. Love them now. Like Jesus, go around doing good to all just like you would want others to do to you. Surprise others with that kind of love intentionally, deliberately . . . now!

Doing unto others includes those who hate us and even those we feel hatred toward. It also includes the "least of these," the poor, the needy, and the overlooked. When teaching about the judgment of the righteous and unrighteous, Jesus goes as far as to say how we treat the "least of these" is how we are treating Him. The true followers of Jesus feed the hungry, visit those in prison, clothe the naked, and care for the sick.

Practicing the Golden Rule both reactively and proactively can be tiring. The Apostle Paul likened it to a farmer patiently and laboriously tending to his fields, waiting for harvest. "Let us not become weary in doing good, for at the proper time we will reap a harvest if we do not give up. Therefore, as we have opportunity, let us do good to all people, especially to those who belong to the family of believers" (Galatians 6:9-10).

May our lives as believers be exemplified by loving others as we would want to be loved. Loving others as Jesus has loved us. That's golden!

Read: Matthew 25:31-46, James 4:17, 1 John 3:18

Reflect: Who am I not treating the way I want to be treated?

Pray: God, loving others is challenging. Help me to learn to love others like I love myself. Teach me to have a heart of compassion and kindness for everyone I meet.

CHAPTER 27

FORGIVE

To err is human, to forgive divine.—Alexander Pope

Some of Jesus's commands tend to get overshadowed by our focus on some of His other teachings. Maybe the best example of that is found in Matthew 6. There are four sentences in that Gospel chapter that might be the most repeated words in the history of the world, known as the Lord's Prayer, "This, then, is how you should pray: 'Our Father in Heaven, hallowed be your name, your kingdom come, your will be done, on earth as it is in Heaven. Give us today our daily bread. And forgive us our debts, as we also have forgiven our debtors. And lead us not into temptation, but deliver us from the evil one'" (Matthew 6:9-13).

But have you ever paid attention to what Jesus said after the "Amen" of that prayer? He continues His teaching with two often-overlooked sentences that are definitely connected with our prayer lives:

> **"For if you forgive other people when they sin against you, your heavenly Father will also forgive you. But if you do not forgive others their sins, your Father will not forgive your sins."** **Matthew 6:14-15**

That's troubling, isn't it? It shakes me (Todd) up. Unless I forgive the sins of others, God will not forgive my sins.

I need to confess to you that when somebody has wronged me, it goes against my nature to forgive them. I just don't want to. It's not instinctive; it's not enjoyable. And I'd like to think it's not necessary or that others wouldn't expect me to do it. I recognize that forgiveness is a divine practice that only comes from God working in me.

Though forgiveness is not easy, Jesus expects it from His followers. The Lord's Prayer is not the only time we see this command; Jesus repeats

Himself time and time again. In Luke 6:37-38, He says, "Do not judge, and you will not be judged. Do not condemn, and you will not be condemned. Forgive, and you will be forgiven. Give, and it will be given to you. A good measure, pressed down, shaken together and running over, will be poured into your lap. For with the measure you use, it will be measured to you."

The scales you use against others—the measuring tape you use to size them up—will be used by God to measure you. And your standard of generosity (or stinginess) will be used by God when He measures out His gifts to you.

You might be asking: But how much is too much to forgive? Does everyone really deserve forgiveness? How many times am I expected to offer this type of forgiveness? Peter asked Jesus a similar question in Matthew 18, questioning how many times we should forgive a person who sins against us. He suggests *maybe* seven times? But Jesus said not seven times but seventy-seven times. That's a big number, and some translations even translate this as seventy times seven!

Jesus continues to help Peter expand his understanding of forgiveness by telling a story of a king with a servant who owed him 10,000 bags of gold. The king demanded the man and his family be sold to pay the debt. But when the man begged for mercy, the king canceled his debt and let him go. The servant left and soon found a fellow servant who owed him a minimal amount of 100 silver coins. Instead of showing the same mercy he had received, he threw the man in prison.

The other servants were outraged and reported all this to the king. The king called out the man's duplicity and lack of mercy on his fellow servant. In his anger, he put the wicked servant in jail to be tortured until he could pay back everything he owed. Jesus explained, "This is how my heavenly Father will treat each of you unless you forgive your brother or sister from your heart" (Matthew 18:35).

Unforgiveness is ultimately a matter of the heart springing from hatred of others. The Apostle John writes, "Anyone who hates a brother or sister is in the darkness, walks around in the darkness. They don't know where they are going because the darkness has blinded them" (I John 2:11).

One of the best examples of this divine forgiveness comes from a famous book written by Corrie Ten Boom called *The Hiding Place*. During WWII in Holland, Corrie, her sister, and her elderly father were arrested for hiding Jews in their home. After their arrest, Corrie never saw or heard from her father again. Betsie, the elder sister and in frailer health, died in the concentration camp. Corrie was eventually released and traveled worldwide sharing the message of God's love and forgiveness.

But one day, her preaching was challenged when she recognized a man in the audience, a former guard from the Ravensbrück concentration camp. She writes about this encounter: "It came back with a rush: the huge room with its harsh overhead lights; the pathetic pile of dresses and shoes in the center of the floor; the shame of walking naked past this man. I could see my sister's frail form ahead of me, ribs sharp beneath the parchment skin. Betsie, how thin you were! Now he was in front of me, hand thrust out: 'A fine message, Fräulein! How good it is to know that, as you say, all our sins are at the bottom of the sea!'"[27]

Corrie froze. The man said that he had become a Christian and knew that God had forgiven him, but he wanted to hear from her that he was forgiven. As she wrestled with what to do, God reminded Corrie of His forgiveness and how He taught us that His forgiveness depends on our forgiveness of others. She reflects, "I knew it not only as a commandment of God, but as a daily experience. Since the end of the war, I had had a home in Holland for victims of Nazi brutality. Those who were able to forgive their former enemies were also able to return to the outside world and rebuild their lives, no matter what the physical scars. Those who nursed their bitterness remained invalids. It was as simple and as horrible as that."[28]

Corrie prayed for help and thrust her hand forward. With that act of obedience, she experienced a healing warmth and was able to offer the man forgiveness with all of her heart. As she stood grasping hands with her former guard, she felt God's love more intensely than ever before.

Many years after Corrie Ten Boom met that prison guard, several women in her church family slandered her and cruelly hurt her. She wrote about this experience, "You would have thought that having forgiven the Nazi guard, this would have been child's play. It wasn't. For weeks I seethed inside, but at last I asked God again to work his miracle in me."[29]

The miracle came when Corrie confessed her struggle with a pastor. The pastor pointed to a church tower and how the bell inside was rung by pulling a rope. "After the sexton lets go of the rope, the bell keeps on swinging. First ding then dong. Slower and slower until there's a final dong and it stops.

I believe the same thing is true of forgiveness. When we forgive someone, we take our hand off the rope. But if we've been tugging at our grievances for a long time, we mustn't be surprised if the old angry thoughts keep coming for a while. They're just the ding-dongs of the old bell slowing down."[30]

Jesus is calling us to forgive as we have been forgiven. How do we do that when we have been grievously hurt? It's hard to forgive a brutal war criminal, but I would say it may be even harder to forgive those who are closest to us.

It is important to remember that forgiveness isn't just about showing mercy to others. It is the antidote for the cancerous bitterness that takes root in our spirits. We become spiritual invalids when we don't forgive. Someone has said, tongue in cheek, "Unforgiveness is like drinking poison, hoping your enemy dies."[31] Another anonymous author wrote, "When you forgive, you heal. When you let go, you grow."

Unforgiveness can eat us up in this life *and* affect our standing before God in the life to come. We've all sinned before God. We've all erred against others. But God has greatly and divinely forgiven us through the cross of Jesus. Now, we can practice the same supernatural mercy that Jesus demonstrated on the cross. Remember, how as they were nailing Him to the tree after He had been betrayed by one of His best friends, deserted by His followers, and after His own countrymen turned Him over to the prison guards, He prayed, "Father, forgive them, for they do not know what they are doing" (Luke 23:34).

Read: Luke 17:3-4, Colossians 3:13, 1 John 4:20-21

Reflect: Do I have unforgiveness and hatred in my heart?

Pray: God, thank You for Your forgiveness. Help me to offer that same divine forgiveness to others. Show me any bitterness or unforgiveness I am holding onto.

CHAPTER 28

Go and Be Reconciled

All this is from God, who reconciled us to himself through Christ and gave us the ministry of reconciliation.
—Paul, the Apostle of Jesus

Have you ever attended a church that looked beautiful and ornate on the outside, with fresh paint, large pillars, beautiful marble steps, and stained-glass windows, and was full of well-dressed churchy people on the inside? But when you looked more closely, you found something was missing. The faith was shallow and artificial; the people were backbiting, spiteful, and altogether un-Christlike. The outward appearance seemed good, but it was only a facade.

In Jesus's day, we see this same problem. The Jewish system of worship that existed for hundreds of years centered around sacrifices, sometimes grain or olive oil, and other times living animals. The purpose of these sacrifices was to keep Israel in a right relationship with God. Unfortunately, for many Jews, those sacrifices became repetitive. Like checking a box, they would go through all the religious rituals but didn't love God or treat people right.

Think about the irony when a person goes through all the motions of religious activity but completely misses the primary purpose of those activities—drawing close to God and people. Let's look at another command where Jesus points us to the priority of relationships. Here, Jesus emphasizes that people are always more important than rituals.

> "So, if you are presenting a sacrifice at the altar in the Temple and you suddenly remember that someone has something against you, leave your sacrifice there at the altar. Go and be reconciled to that person. Then come and offer your sacrifice to God." **Matthew 5:23-24 NLT**

Consider the significance of the sacrifice in this scenario. Every time they sinned, each person in Israel, whether wealthy or poor, was required to slaughter a living animal to repair their relationship with God. The sacrifice was an atonement for their offense before God. Hebrews 9:22 explains, "For without the shedding of blood, there is no forgiveness." To that person at the altar, the sacrifice was of tremendous importance. Yet, God is saying, *Stop. Go and fix the problem you have with someone else, then come back and finish your sacrifice.*

While studying this command, I (Stacey) started pondering the value of human life and asked my wife, "Honey, have you ever wondered if you got kidnapped what people would be willing to pay to get you back?" We just sat there for a minute, and she looked at me and said, "I don't know. How much would you pay for me?" There was only one answer to that question: Everything!

When we consider our value, even more important than wondering what ransom people would be willing to pay for us, we need to consider what ransom God would pay. Peter gives us the answer in I Peter 1:18-19 NLT: "For you know that God paid a ransom to save you from the empty life you inherited from your ancestors. And it was not paid with mere gold or silver, which lose their value. It was the precious blood of Christ, the sinless, spotless Lamb of God." We are priceless treasures to our Father in Heaven, valuable enough to be purchased by the blood of His only Son Jesus.

This coin has two sides. If you are precious and valuable to God, this must also mean that any person you are upset or angry with is just as valuable and precious in His sight. God is calling us to stop ignoring the conflict, the brokenness, and the bitterness, and seek reconciliation because people are priceless to Him.

You may have noticed Jesus's words are aimed at the guilty party: "If you are presenting a sacrifice at the altar in the temple and you suddenly remember that somebody has something against you . . ." The person about to offer a sacrifice has done something to offend somebody. So, does this mean this command only applies to those who have done the hurting?

When we look at the larger context of Scripture, we can confidently answer *no*. Jesus places responsibility on both the victim and the perpetrator of the sin. In Mark 11:25, He said, "And when you stand praying, if you hold anything against anyone, forgive them, so that your Father in Heaven may forgive you your sins." In Romans 12:18, Paul says, "If it is possible, as far as it depends on you, live at peace with everyone." We should work hard at peace and reconciliation and do everything within our power to make things right.

I recently heard a testimony that demonstrates the power of reconciliation. In 1992, while driving drunk, Joe Avila took the life of Amy Wall, a 17-year-old girl. After being booked for second-degree murder and spending a few days in jail, Joe started looking for a way to kill himself. Then, a chaplain visited and shared these profound words, "Joe, Christ died on the cross even for what you did five days ago." Joe decided to accept this forgiveness and follow Jesus. He took responsibility for his actions, pleaded guilty, and spent the next seven and half years in prison.

After his release, Joe was welcomed warmly into a church family who willingly displayed God's forgiveness. Then, Amy's brother Derek asked to meet him. Joe had been praying for reconciliation with Amy's family for years, so he agreed to meet. Derek told Joe about Amy and how many things they did together. He also shared that, at one time, he thought Joe was a monster who deserved the electric chair. Joe expressed how sorry he was for what he had done and how he hoped Derek could forgive him one day.

A few weeks later, Amy's dad Rick requested a meeting. During the meeting, Rick extended forgiveness before Joe even asked for it. Then Joe spent time with Amy's mom. Together, they watched a video of Amy's life, and Joe got to know Amy, how precious she was, and what a tragedy happened when he took her life. Later, Derek and Joe were asked to participate in a restored justice council. Joe recalls that, during this gathering of several hundred people, he saw a gentleman come directly over to him. It was Rick. Rick grabbed and hugged him and said, "I love you, Joe." Joe had killed his daughter, yet Rick was able to hug him and say I love you. What a picture of reconciliation![32]

Christian brothers and sisters, Jesus is reminding us that the way we treat each other, even in hardship, communicates to the whole world who He is. Like Amy's family, when we love with the same sacrificial love that Christ loves us, we share the message of hope and forgiveness.

In Matthew 5:14-16, Jesus compares our impact on the world to light: "You are the light of the world. A town built on a hill cannot be hidden. Neither do people light a lamp and put it under a bowl. Instead, they put it on its stand, and it gives light to everyone in the house. In the same way, let your light shine before others, that they may see your good deeds and glorify your Father in Heaven."

Great harm is done when the church only cleans up the outside and continues to bicker, fight, and live in discord. The world will always look for an excuse to discredit the church, and when we don't love each other, we give them good reason. However, when a church lives out its faith in genuine love, peace, and forgiveness, it shines like a light into the darkness, and we become all we were called to be.

Read: Hosea 6:6, John 17:20-21, 1 Peter 3:7

Reflect: Is there anyone I need to make peace with?

Pray: God, forgive me when I make following You a ritual without allowing You to transform my heart. Help me to be a peacemaker and shine Your light and love.

# SECTION 5

MINDSET

For the mouth speaks what the heart is full of. A good man brings good things out of the good stored up in him, and an evil man brings evil things out of the evil stored up in him.

Matthew 12:34-35

CHAPTER 29

STORE UP TREASURES IN HEAVEN

> *If I find in myself a desire which no experience in this world can satisfy, the most probable explanation is that I was made for another world . . . I must keep alive in myself the desire for my true country, which I shall not find until after death. I must never let it get snowed under or turned aside; I must make it the main object of life to press on to that country and to help others to do the same.*
> —C.S. Lewis, Mere Christianity

In 2014, a couple was walking around their Nevada property. They passed a familiar tree with a rusty old tin can sticking out of the ground they had always thought might be a grave marker. This time, their curiosity got the best of them, and they looked closer. As they brushed away the dirt, the can disintegrated, revealing the old coins hidden inside. The next day, they discovered eight more cans filled with pure gold American Double Eagle coins. Unsure of what to do, they hid the coins under their wood pile. Eventually, they called in experts who confirmed all 1,400 coins were indeed theirs. Since that discovery, they have been slowly selling the coins and have made over 11 million dollars. What a find![33]

You have to wonder about the original owner of those coins. What paranoia did they feel to place all this treasure into tin cans and bury it? No bank was good enough, no vault was secure enough, and no friend was trusted enough. Instead, the coins were hidden by the tree until the day they were needed, but that day never came. This person died with their treasure buried in the dirt for some future stranger to come and unearth.

In Matthew 6, Jesus gave us an eternal perspective on our treasures and our money:

> **"Do not store up for yourselves treasures on earth, where moths and vermin destroy, and where thieves break in and steal. But store up for yourselves treasures in heaven, where moths and vermin do not destroy, and where thieves do not break in and steal. For where your treasure is, there your heart will be also."** — Matthew 6:19-21

I (Stacey) don't believe Jesus's command here was given to prevent people from saving money responsibly. Rather, I believe this command was given because far too many people are building up treasures as though this life is all there is. While it's wise to put money away for future uncertainties, we don't want to be like the Nevada man, hoarding our earthly treasure out of fear or self-preservation.

James reminds us in James 4:14: "Why, you do not know what will happen tomorrow. What is your life? You are a mist that appears for a little while and then vanishes." We can forget way too quickly that this world is a temporary place. At some point, every person reading these words will vanish in a physical sense. But our souls will continue into eternity.

This life is filled with so many tangible and wonderful distractions that steal our view away from God. I remember many times coming out of the store with candy to surprise my kids. I expected that when I handed the gift over to my children, they would actually share it with me. But isn't it amazing how quickly the gift becomes "mine"? In His goodness, God gave us touch, smell, sight, and taste to enjoy this wonderful world, but too often, we fall in love with the gifts of God and forget the Gift-giver altogether.

In a parable about spiritual growth, Jesus compared our hearts to soil where seed is planted. The kind of soil you have will determine whether the seed of God's Kingdom grows and thrives or struggles and fails. Jesus explained that some hearts are like thorny and weedy soil. "The seed falling among the thorns refers to someone who hears the word, but the worries of this life and the deceitfulness of wealth choke the word, making it unfruitful" (Matthew 13:22).

In Luke 12, Jesus talked about a rich man who decided to build bigger barns to store up for the future. He planned to have an easy life full of food, drink, and merriment. But then he died suddenly, unable to take any of these earthy treasures with him. It reminds me of a story about a man who was a real cheapskate. Just before he died, he asked his wife to put all of his money in the casket so he could take it with him to the afterlife. Before the casket was closed, his wife slipped in an envelope. When questioned, the wife confirmed she had indeed put all the man's money in the casket with him. She explained that she had gathered all the money in her bank account and then written him a check.

While humorous, this story underscores the truth that we cannot jam our treasures into our casket and somehow transport them into our Heavenly home. Since we cannot take our physical treasures with us into eternity, we need to carefully consider how we can store up treasures in Heaven.

After telling the story of the rich man and his barns, in Luke 12:32-33, Jesus said, "Do not be afraid, little flock, for your Father has been pleased to give you the kingdom. Sell your possessions and give to the poor. Provide purses for yourselves that will not wear out, a treasure in Heaven that will never fail, where no thief comes near and no moth destroys." Over and over in Scripture, we're taught that those who sacrificially, joyfully give to others will be rewarded. In Luke 16:9 Jesus said, "Use your worldly resources to benefit others and make friends. Then, when your possessions are gone, they will welcome you to an eternal home."

When a wealthy young man asked Jesus how to receive eternal life, Jesus told him, "If you want to be perfect, go, sell your possessions and give it to the poor, and you will have treasure in Heaven. Then come, follow me" (Matthew 19:21). As we invest both time and resources in the people that God brings into our life, we are literally building treasure in Heaven.

But as important as it is to invest in people, there is no greater investment and no better return on our time than being rich in our relationship with God. Jesus didn't just tell the wealthy young man to give all his money to the poor; He also said, *come and follow Me*. If we give all our money away but fail to follow Jesus Christ, we have missed the mark and are only exercising worldly social justice. It's when our generosity to those in need is combined with a vibrant daily relationship with God that we begin to build eternal treasure that will never be taken or stolen from us.

Friends, when you take an honest inventory of your life, where are you building your treasure? Jesus gave us the perfect example of an earthly life focused on eternity. Hebrews 12:2 describes His mindset: "For the joy set before him he endured the cross, scorning its shame, and sat down at the right hand of the throne of God." Jesus knew that a better place and a better time was coming when He would sit beside His Father in the throne room. And through His death on the cross, He adopted us as sons and daughters, co-heirs to join Him in His inheritance.

Listen to what Paul says in Romans 8:17 NLT: "And since we are his children, we are also his heirs. In fact, together with Christ we are heirs of God's glory." What a treasure! What a beautiful future that awaits us. I Corinthians 2:9 NLT promises, "No eye has seen, no ear has heard, and no mind has imagined what God has prepared for those who love him." We cannot fully grasp what God has in store for us. But by our simple faith and obedience, investing in people and God, we know we are storing up for that grand and wonderful future.

Read: Philippians 3:7, 1 Timothy 6:18-19, 1 Peter 2:11

Reflect: What am I doing today to store up treasure in Heaven?

Pray: God, I look forward to spending eternity with You. Forgive me when I get so focused on today that I forget about You and Your Kingdom. Show me how to make eternal investments today.

CHAPTER 30

Beware of Covetousness

> *Covetousness is the greatest of monsters, as well as the root of all evil.*
> —William Penn

As I worked through all of Jesus's commands, I (Todd) studied topics I don't remember preaching or teaching before. One of those is covetousness. In Luke 12, Jesus warns us about this important topic:

> **"And He said to them, 'Take heed, and beware of covetousness: for one's life does not consist in the abundance of things he possesses.'"** **Luke 12: 15 NKJV**

Let's start with the basics. What does the word *covet* mean? I looked at the dictionary and found that *covet* means *eager or excessive desire, especially for wealth or possessions.*[34] Some Bible translations substitute the term *greed* or *the love of money*, but it's all the same. Covetousness is dangerous, deceptive, and something that can destroy our lives.

Though often overlooked, covetousness is addressed in the Ten Commandments. Exodus 20:17 records this law written on stone by the finger of God: "You shall not covet your neighbor's house. You shall not covet your neighbor's wife, or his male or female servant, his ox or donkey, or anything that belongs to your neighbor."

In Mark 7:21-23 NKJV, Jesus includes covetousness among those awful sins that defile us: "For from within, out of the heart of men, proceed evil thoughts, adulteries, fornications, murders, thefts, covetousness, wickedness, deceit, lewdness, an evil eye, blasphemy, pride, foolishness. All these evil things come from within and defile a man." Defilement means to make what was once clean, unclean, or what was once pure, impure. Covetousness is a corruption of perfection and beauty.

The Apostle Paul likened covetousness to idolatry. "For this you know, that no fornicator, unclean person, nor covetous man, who is an idolater, has any inheritance in the kingdom of Christ and God" (Ephesians 5:5 NKJV). For the Jewish people, idolatry meant turning their back on God and making themselves new gods of stone, wood, silver, or gold. After they fashioned an idol, they would kneel down, pray to it, and bring offerings. That's crazy, isn't it? Yes, and Paul would say it is the same for us when we covet! Anything we worship, anything we desire more than God, is idolatry. It doesn't have to be a statue made of gold. It can be the money in the bank or your neighbor's house that's bigger and better than yours.

Consider the church with its hundreds of different denominations. Isn't it a shame that most of the church growth in America comes from division rather than multiplication? We get mad at each other, we don't agree with each other scripturally, and we split and split again and build our own exclusive buildings. My goodness, isn't that a kind of idolatry born from covetousness? And this division within the church is not new.

James, the brother of Jesus, became the first pastor of the first church in Jerusalem. The book of Acts tells us that on the day that the church was formed, there were three thousand baptisms. Soon after that, the arguments and fighting began. Listen to these wise words from James, true of the church in Jerusalem and true of the church today: "What causes fights and quarrels among you? Don't they come from your desires that battle within you? You desire but do not have, so you kill. You covet but you cannot get what you want, so you quarrel and fight. You do not have because you do not ask God. When you ask, you do not receive, because you ask with wrong motives, that you may spend what you get on your pleasures" (James 4:1-3).

What is at the heart of division and fighting? Greed. Covetousness. The longing for stuff and pleasure. It is idol-building right inside God's church.

Leo Tolstoy was a famous Russian author, perhaps one of the most famous authors in the history of the world. He lived a rough and sinful life until he became a disciple of Jesus. Read this summary of one of his short stories "How Much Land Does a Man Need?". You'll recognize Jesus's teaching in it.

> Tolstoy once wrote a story about a successful peasant farmer that wasn't satisfied with his lot. He wanted more of everything. One

day he received an intriguing offer. For one thousand rubles he could buy all the land he could walk around in one day. The only catch in the deal was that he had to be back at his starting point at sundown or the deal was off. Early the next morning he started out walking at a fast pace but by mid-day he was very tired, but he kept going, covering more and more ground well into the afternoon. Then he realized that his greed had taken him far from the starting point, he quickened his pace and as the sun began to sink low in the sky, he began to run knowing that if he didn't make it back by sundown the opportunity to become an even bigger landowner would be lost. As the sun began to sink below the horizon, he came within sight of the finish line. Gasping for breath, his heart pounding, he called upon every bit of strength left in his body and staggered across the line just before the sun disappeared. He immediately collapsed, blood streaming from his mouth and in a few minutes he was dead. Afterwards his servants dug a grave, it was not much over six feet long and three feet wide.[35]

Covetousness is a great monster. The more attention we give it, the more we feed it, the bigger it grows, and the more powerful it becomes. Eventually, it will kill us unless we destroy it first. In Colossians 3:5 NKJV, Paul instructs us to "put to death your members which are on the earth: fornication, uncleanness, passion, evil desire, and covetousness, which is idolatry."

So, where do we start? It's easy to say "thou shalt not covet" but how do we practically quit building idols? Let me give you three keys from Scriptures to help us overcome covetousness in our lives.

1. Be content with what you have: "But godliness with contentment is great gain. For we brought nothing into the world, and we can take nothing out of it. But if we have food and clothing, we will be content with that. Those who want to get rich fall into temptation and a trap and into many foolish and harmful desires that plunge people into ruin and destruction. For the love of money is a root of all kinds of evil. Some people, eager for money, have wandered from the faith and pierced themselves with many griefs" (1 Timothy 6:6-10).

2. Seek God's Kingdom: "But seek first the kingdom of God and his righteousness and everything you need will be given to you" (Matthew 6:33 ESV).

3. Love one another: "Let no debt remain outstanding, except the continuing debt to love one another, for whoever loves others has fulfilled the law. The commandments, 'You shall not commit adultery, you shall not murder, you shall not steal, you shall not covet, and whatever other commands there may be, are summed up in this one command: Love your neighbor as yourself.' Love does no harm to a neighbor. Therefore, love is the fulfillment of the law" (Romans 13:8-10).

Friend, are you exhausted from building idols and chasing after what other people have? If so, it's time to slay the monster, destroy covetousness, and be passionately consumed with service in God's Kingdom.

Read: Psalm 119:36, Luke 12:13-21, Romans 7:7-11, 1 Peter 2:9-12

Reflect: Where is covetousness gaining ground in your life? What idols are you building?

Pray: God, forgive me for the times I covet, fight, and quarrel with others trying to come out on top. Help me replace greed with contentment and love.

CHAPTER 31

DO NOT WORRY

When we allow worries to dominate us, we're actually saying that God can't be trusted to take care of us. But He can be trusted!
—Billy Graham

Are you a worrier? Or are you married to a worrier?

I (Todd) heard this story that may apply to some of you. For years, a woman had trouble getting to sleep at night out of fear of burglars. One night, her now-elderly husband heard a noise in the house and went downstairs to investigate. When he found a burglar, he greeted him, "Good evening. I am so glad to meet you. Please, come upstairs and meet my wife. She's been waiting 25 years for you."

The truth is that most things we worry, fret, and wring our hands about will never happen. Worry is like a rocking chair; it gives you something to do but doesn't get you anywhere. Instead, it can lead to anxiety and crippling fear. Jesus had a lot to say about worrying over the stuff of life. As we look at what may be a very familiar passage, let's try to understand what Jesus meant when He told us not to worry:

> **"Therefore I tell you, do not worry about your life, what you will eat or drink; or about your body, what you will wear. Is not life more than food, and the body more than clothes?"**
> **Matthew 6:25**

Jesus pointed to the birds of the air, which God feeds, and the flowers of the field, which God clothes, as examples of why we should not worry. He continued by saying, "So do not worry, saying, 'What shall we eat?' or 'What shall we drink, or what shall we wear?' For the pagans run after all these things, and your heavenly Father knows that you need them. But seek first his kingdom and his righteousness, and all these things will be given to you as well. Therefore, do not worry about tomorrow, for tomorrow will worry about itself. Each day has enough trouble of its own" (Matthew 6:31-34).

I wonder if Jesus's original listeners recalled how God provided for the Israelites in the desert. Theologians think there may have been two million people who, without much warning, got up in the middle of the night, journeyed to the desert, and stayed there for 40 years. Manna showed up every morning, quail blew in with the wind, water flowed from the rock, and their clothes never wore out!

We serve the same God, yet we wring our hands, worrying —will there be enough? Will He take care of me? Does He care about me?

In the late 90s, I owned a business. It wasn't a very good business, and I wasn't a good businessman, evidenced by the fact that I didn't make much money for eight years. It was a tough season, and my wife Karen and I prayed many prayers. That winter, I was preparing to travel overseas and leave Karen at home running the business and caring for our two boys. Karen was worried as the trip got closer, but I kept telling her that God would provide.

Two days before my flight, our only car broke down. I went outside, prayed God's promises, and turned the key—nothing. I raised the hood and gazed intently at the engine like I had seen other men do—nothing. Karen begged me to keep trying, so I found a screwdriver, lifted the hood again, and started banging—nothing. I went back inside, reported to Karen that we just needed to trust God, and started packing.

Later that evening, our doorbell rang. It was our neighbors, looking very serious. I was sure something was wrong, so I invited them to sit in the living room. The husband had a black box in his lap. After a few minutes, he spoke up and said, "Yesterday, God told my wife to do something for you. She told God she would only do it if God spoke the same thing to me without her saying anything. This morning, when I got my coffee and saw you out the window banging on your engine with a screwdriver, God spoke to me. So, my wife and I brought this box with the keys, papers, and an owner's manual for our less-than-one-year-old car. It's yours."

We all started crying. We understood that God was working. After our kind neighbors left, Karen and I took the boys out to our new car, which had leather seats and still smelled new. I told the boys, "I never want you to forget God cares for His children. God takes care of His children."

Please don't hear from this story that we all get new cars. What I want you to remember is that God loves you, He knows what you need, and He knows how to fill up what's missing in your life.

It is important to note that Jesus is not teaching us that if we are good Christians, we'll never have anything to worry about. Along with this command not to worry, Jesus also said trouble is coming. Trouble is a part of life. Each day has trouble, which means tomorrow has trouble banked up. We all could tell countless stories of life's sickness, loss, and discouragement.

What Jesus is saying is that there are more important concerns than food, drink, and clothes. The pagans run after that stuff, but God the Father will provide for you when you give attention to what's really important. And He tells us what is most important: to seek His kingdom and His righteousness.

Jesus said, "Blessed are those who hunger and thirst for righteousness, for they will be filled" (Matthew 5:6). Righteousness means to act in accordance with divine or moral law, free from guilt or sin, morally right or justifiable. The antidote to worry, care, and anxiety, no matter what the source, is that you intentionally seek God's Kingdom with your face toward Heaven, like the Jewish people in the desert who had their faces set toward the Promised Land. We need to be intentionally dedicated to living righteous lives.

The Apostle Paul wrote this in Romans 14:17-18: "For the kingdom of God is not a matter of eating and drinking, but of righteousness, peace and joy in the Holy Spirit, because anyone who serves Christ in this way is pleasing to God and receives human approval." Listen to these blessings: righteousness, peace, and joy in the Holy Spirit. What a blessing to have peace and joy. Worry always robs you of both.

I love Psalm 85:10, which says, "Love and faithfulness meet together; righteousness and peace kiss each other." The Psalmist personifies righteousness and peace as two people who love each other, go on a date, and kiss each other. From this picture, we see that there is no peace without righteousness, and there is no righteousness without peace.

If you're reading this today lacking peace, it's not because your bank account doesn't have enough money or because of any other external problem. The real reason you're lacking peace is because you're lacking faith. Your mind is not set on Heaven but on all the challenges surrounding you. But if you will seek His righteousness and His kingdom, there will be peace and joy in the Holy Spirit waiting for you. Yes, trouble will still come, but you will be a different person with a different attitude and a new perspective.

Read: Psalm 119:1-3, Colossians 1:12-14, Luke 12:32-34

Reflect: What am I worrying about today?

Pray: God, thank You for caring for the birds and the flowers. Thank You for taking care of me. Help me to replace worry with the righteousness, peace, and joy of Your Spirit.

CHAPTER 32

DO NOT BE AFRAID

Let me assert from my firm belief, that the only thing we have to fear is fear itself—nameless, unreasoning, unjustified terror which paralyzes needed efforts to convert retreat into advance.
—*President Franklin Roosevelt*

A few years ago, I (Stacey) visited one of our church's mission partners, Central India Christian Mission, in the heart of India. It's a wonderful organization that has done so much good to advance the Kingdom of God for thousands and thousands of people. As we ministered in India, I was with my wife, two of my children, seven women from our church, and interpreters to walk us through a culture so very different from our own. One afternoon, when we were leaving the hotel, three men approached us carrying two round wicker baskets and a large feed sack.

The interpreters said, "You guys will love this. They want to show you what they have in the baskets, and then you can give them a little tip; it would just bless them so much." So, we gathered around these men, watching as they sat the baskets down. Then the lid popped off, and two king cobras came lifting right up. The snakes were swaying and dancing as the men sat cross-legged in front of the baskets, playing the flute. We were staring, stunned, feeling like we were just dropped into an Indiana Jones movie.

Meanwhile, behind these snake charmers, the third man was still grasping a bulging feed sack, leaving our group to wonder uneasily what he held. When they finally asked us if we wanted to see what was inside, even though I was thinking no way, we just stood there as two guys grabbed each side of the feed sack. Then, one man reached down to pull out a six-foot python they had proudly caught that morning. When they asked, "Who wants to hold it?" most of us backed up laughing nervously, but one young lady, Carmen, stepped forward. As she stood there, tense, hands clenched with that snake laid across her shoulders, she said something I will never forget, "My dad taught me since I was a little girl that when I experience fear, don't ever run away, instead turn and run towards it."

Those words stuck with me because fear is such a present, daily reality in our lives. Sometimes, fear causes us to run away; other times, it freezes us in indecision. Fear can be based on reality or invisible perceptions. Regardless of where our fear originates from, it is a powerful thing that influences what we do, who we interact with, and how we live.

The Bible discusses fear from Genesis to Revelation. It's notable that in the Garden of Eden when the perfect man and perfect woman chose to sin, they experienced two powerful emotions for the first time in human history. First, they felt shame, and immediately following shame, they experienced fear. Since that day, fear has lurked in the dark corners of all our lives.

Revelation, the final book of the Bible, not only records history, but it also records things that haven't happened yet, things that may occur in our time. We read about a world that is collapsing under the weight of sin and godlessness, moving towards its climatic end, and a church experiencing hardship and persecution. When the book opens, Jesus appears to the Apostle John in a vision. John recognizes His risen Lord speaking to him and falls to the ground, paralyzed with fear. I love how Jesus responds to John's fear.

> **"Then he placed his right hand on me and said, 'Do not be afraid. I am the First and the Last. I am the Living One; I was dead, and now look, I am alive for ever and ever! And I hold the keys of death and Hades.'"   Revelation 1:17-18**

This command, "Do not fear," echoes throughout the Bible. Almost eighteen hundred years earlier, God would say to Abraham, the father of Israel, "Do not be afraid, Abram, for I will protect you" (Genesis 15:1 NLT). Years later, as Israel entered into the Promised Land, God would reassure a new leader to His people named Joshua, "Have I not commanded you? Be strong and courageous. Do not be afraid, and do not be discouraged, for the LORD your God will be with you wherever you go" (Joshua 1:9).

In all of Scripture, I have found only one exception to this commandment. In Matthew 10:28, Jesus said, "Do not be afraid of those who kill the body but cannot kill the soul. Rather, be afraid of the One who can destroy both soul and body in hell." We're commanded to fear God; in fact, the fear of the Lord is the beginning of all wisdom. Every other fear that plagues our minds falls under this command: "Do not be afraid."

In some ways, the command not to be afraid can seem a little bit out of touch with reality. There are a thousand things in every moment of our lives that give us reason to be fearful. It seems every corner of the globe has some war, strife, or hardship. When I speak to mental health professionals, they report that depression, anxiety, hurt, and anger are rampant.

However, as out of touch as it may feel, no one knows better what it's like to be in the pressure cooker of this world while living out your faith than Jesus Christ Himself. Remember, in the last chapter, we looked at His promise that states we will have trouble in this world? While Christ walked on this earth, He was a man who was acquainted with every hardship, hatred, and evil. He would tell His followers in John 15:18: "If the world hates you, keep in mind that it hated me first."

Fellow believers, following Jesus does not guarantee security and safety. If we return to Revelation, only a few verses after Jesus comforted His friend John with the words, "Do not be afraid," He shares some hard words for the future church. We are told we will suffer persecution, some will be put in prison, and some will even be put to death (Revelation 2:10). While this warning may have been written two thousand years ago, it is still relevant today as tens of thousands of our brothers and sisters all over the world actively face this type of persecution.

In Matthew 24:9-12, Jesus describes what happens to the hearts of immature and uncommitted believers at the end of time: "Then you will be handed over to be persecuted and put to death, and you will be hated by all nations because of me. At that time many will turn away from the faith and will betray and hate each other, and many false prophets will appear and deceive many people. Because of the increase of wickedness, the love of most will grow cold."

Friends, I pray that this verse does not describe us. When the spirit of fear shouts, "Run and hide, blend in, protect your comfort and vitality at all costs," what will we do?

In Romans 8:31, Paul gives us the alternative to fear by asking, "What, then, shall we say in response to these things? If God is for us, who can be against us?" Paul continues by reminding us that Jesus, who died for us, is also interceding before God for us. There is no trouble, persecution, or danger of any kind that can separate us from His love. Through the powerful love of Jesus, we are more than conquerors, not only in the present but for all time.

One of my favorite images of bravery is David against Goliath. As that young shepherd boy strode out into the field before all the Philistine army, the armies of Israel stood behind him, terrified and dismayed. As David walked away from the safety of his countrymen toward Goliath, he said these words: "This day the Lord will deliver you into my hands, and I'll strike you down and cut off your head. This very day I will give the carcasses of the Philistine army to the birds and the wild animals, and the whole world will know that there is a God in Israel. All those gathered here will know that it is not by sword or spear that the Lord saves; for the battle is the Lord's, and he will give all of you into our hands" (I Samuel 17:46-47).

After those brave words, when the Philistine giant moved forward to attack him, the Bible says that David ran quickly toward the battle line to meet him.

Let's learn from David. Today is not the time for us to cower in fear. It is time to face our fears. It is time for us to advance God's Kingdom by the power of the Holy Spirit. Remember Carmen with the serpent on her shoulders, choosing to run toward fear? We can run toward fear because we know the battle has been won. Let's call out to the fear that has been hiding and reverberating in our minds with the truth of the Gospel. We are set free. We are more than conquerors. By the blood of Jesus, through the power of the cross, we can say, "No, Satan, not today, not me, not this church."

Read: John 14:27, 2 Timothy 1:7, Hebrews 13:6, 1 Peter 3:14

Reflect: What fear am I allowing to paralyze me?

Pray: Jesus, I am a conqueror through You. Help me to run toward fear and not away from it. Help me to claim Your victory.

CHAPTER 33

Ask, Seek, Knock

"The great value of persistent prayer is not that God will hear us, but that we will finally hear God." —William McGill

Jesus taught us that persistence and prayer go hand in hand. He instructs us to pray and keep on praying:

"Ask and it will be given to you; seek and you will find; knock and the door will be opened to you. For everyone who asks receives; the one who seeks finds; and to the one who knocks, the door will be opened." Matthew 7:7-8

Persistence by definition is *firm, even stubborn continuance in a course of action in spite of difficulty or opposition.*[36] Let me share one of my (Todd's) favorite personal stories about persistent prayer.

Five-year-old Johnny surprised his parents one night at dinner as he blurted out, "I want a baby brother. What do I need to do around here to help get a baby brother?" Johnny's father looked at his wife, winked, turned to Johnny, and said, "I'll guarantee you, if you pray every day for the next two months, God will give you a brother." For about a month, Johnny faithfully knelt by his bed and prayed every night, but when he didn't see anything happening, he got bored and discouraged from praying. Some of his friends in the neighborhood advised, "Johnny, it doesn't work that way; you don't just pray for a baby brother, and whammo, God gives you one." So, Johnny quit praying.

About one month later, Johnny's mom went to the hospital. After returning home, she called Johnny into her bedroom. He walked in cautiously and found his mom lying on the bed with a bundle wrapped in a blanket. His dad said, "Come here, Johnny, look at this." His dad peeled the blanket down to reveal two little babies. He said, "Johnny, you have twin brothers. Look how good God's been to you. Aren't you glad you prayed the way you did?" Johnny responded, "Yeah, but aren't you glad I stopped when I did?"

Jesus continued His teaching on prayer by comparing God to an earthly Father: "Which of you, if your son asks for bread, will give him a stone? Or if he asks for a fish, will give him a snake? If you then, though you are evil, know how to give good gifts to your children, how much more will your Father in Heaven give good gifts to those who ask him!" (Matthew 7:9-11).

While prayer does not always feel as straightforward or simple as we would like, we can trust that God is a good Father who loves and cares for His children. It's easy to mistake Jesus's teaching here for sounding like a genie in a bottle—you pick up the prayer bottle, rub it, make your request, and then the genie answers. But that is not quite how prayer works, and it is not how God works. Let's look at the greater context of these three words: *ask*, *seek*, and *knock*.

1. ASK, AND IT WILL BE GIVEN TO YOU.

Jesus intends for us to ask and ask consistently. Billy Graham said, "Heaven is full of answers to prayers to which no one ever bothered to ask."[37] We should come again and again, bringing our petitions to God, believing He will hear us. 1 John 5:14-15 says, "This is the confidence we have in approaching God: that if we ask anything according to his will, he hears us. And if we know that he hears us—whatever we ask—we know that we have what we asked of him."

When we ask, we should make sure our desires are Biblical and that we are not asking with selfish, fleshy motives. We also need to recognize that sometimes God's answer is *no*. No, because God wants what is best for us and what will magnify Himself.

The Apostle Paul was beaten up by his hard life; he was physically broken and ailing. Paul prayed three times, deep wrestling prayers that his "thorn in the flesh" would go away. Instead of granting a release from the struggle, God responded, "My grace is sufficient for you, for my power is made perfect in weakness" (2 Corinthians 12:9). Jesus Himself, on the night of His arrest, knowing the cross was coming, prayed in agony three times, wrestling with God until He was sweating drops of blood to take the coming cup away from Him. But He also prayed, "May your will be done" (Matthew 26:42).

Sometimes, God will put you on a hard path of sacrifice you don't want to go on, a time of giving something up, grieving, or crying out for release. But like Jesus, the mature Christian, trusting their Heavenly Father, finally relents and says, "May Your will be done."

2. SEEK, AND YOU WILL FIND.

When Jesus's original audience heard the word *seek*, they would immediately connect it to the Old Testament historical context. Right before the people of Israel entered the Promised Land, Moses instilled in them the importance of seeking God: "But if from there you seek the Lord your God, you will find him if you seek him with all your heart and with all your soul" (Deuteronomy 4:29). David would say in Psalm 34:10, "those who seek the Lord lack no good thing." Then, hundreds of years later, the Prophet Jeremiah would echo this truth: "You will seek me and find me when you seek me with all your heart" (Jeremiah 29:13).

Jesus continually encouraged people to seek God, His Kingdom, and His righteousness. In our prayers, the first thing we should ask ourselves is "Am I seeking God, principally, primarily? Are my priorities His Kingdom and His righteousness?" It is only when I seek God with all my heart that I will find Him.

3. KNOCK, AND THE DOOR WILL BE OPENED.

In Luke 11, Jesus told a parable that teaches us to pray with shameless audacity. He illustrates this by asking His audience what would happen if they went to a friend at midnight and asked for three loaves of bread because they had a visitor and didn't have any food to offer. Most likely, the friend would say, "Go away. My door is locked, and I am not getting up." But Jesus continues, "I tell you even though he will not get up and give you the bread because of friendship, yet because of your shameless audacity he will surely get up and give you as much as you need" (Luke 11:8).

Luke continues by echoing Matthew's instructions on prayer: ask, seek, knock. Shameless audacity is when we are not ashamed to keep coming, keep asking, and keep knocking until the door opens.

Then Luke adds additional insight about God's loving care of His children: "How much more will your Father in Heaven give the Holy Spirit to those who ask him!" (Luke 11:13). The Holy Spirit is the very best gift God could give us because the Holy Spirit leads us in the truth, helps us to know the way, reveals deception, shows us God's will, and comforts us in our loss. In John 16:13, we learn, "But when he, the Spirit of truth, comes, he will guide you into all truth. He will not speak on his own; he will speak only what he hears, and he will tell you what is yet to come."

The Holy Spirit guides us in truth, and He also helps us to pray. If you're like me, sometimes you don't know what to pray or how to pray. Your circumstances are convoluted, your heart and mind are at odds, or you are submersed in grief so that you don't know what to ask for. That's where the Holy Spirit comes in. The Apostle Paul writes in Romans 8:26, "In the same way, the Spirit helps us in our weakness. We do not know what we ought to pray for, but the Spirit himself intercedes for us through wordless groans."

Like me, some of you may have grown up praying to God, our Heavenly Father, and occasionally praying to Jesus, but never learning to pray to the Holy Spirit. Only in recent years have I prayed, "Holy Spirit, coach me, show me, help me here. Holy Spirit, intercede. I know you will take my request to the throne, and you will ache and groan on my behalf to the Father." I don't know if it exactly correlates with James's teaching, "You don't have because you don't ask God" (James 4:2), but I wonder if we have grieved the Holy Spirit because we never talk to Him.

There are many different needs that we pray about with persistence. If you are a parent, one of those is for your children. From the time they're born, we cry out for them. When they go off the rails in seasons of rebellion, we knock hard on the door of Heaven. I want to encourage you with this story of praying with shameless audacity. Jim Cymbala, pastor of the Brooklyn Tabernacle, writes in his book *Fresh Wind, Fresh Fire* about a season when his daughter Chrissy turned away from God and her family in rebellion.

During this rebellious season, another pastor advised Jim that now that Chrissy was 18, he needed to let go and accept her decisions. He said that something deep within him began to cry out, knowing he could never accept his daughter turning away from the Lord. He writes, "God strongly impressed on me to stop crying, screaming or talking to anyone else about Chrissy. I was to converse with no one but God, in fact, I knew I should have no further contact with Chrissy until God acted. I was just to believe and obey and trust what I had preached so often: **Call upon me in the day of trouble, says the Lord and I will answer you.** So, I began to pray with an intensity and a growing faith as never before.

Whatever bad news I would receive about Chrissy I kept interceding and actually began praising God for what I knew he would do soon."[38]

Then, one February, during a prayer meeting, a spiritually sensitive woman passed him a note that said she felt impressed they should stop the meeting and pray for Chrissy. Despite a bit of hesitation, the note rang true, and Jim asked the group to join him in praying for Chrissy. Thirty hours later, Jim's wife Carol came upstairs to tell him Chrissy was at their house and wanted to see him. Jim shares,

> As I came around the corner, I saw my daughter on the kitchen floor rocking on her hands and knees, sobbing. Cautiously I spoke her name, "Chrissy". She grabbed my pant leg and began pouring out her anguish, "Daddy, daddy, I have sinned against God, I have sinned against myself, I sinned against you and mommy, please forgive me." My vision was as clouded by tears as hers, I pulled her up from the floor and held her close and we cried together. Suddenly she drew back, "Daddy, who's been praying for me?" she asked. I replied, "What do you mean Chrissy?" "On Tuesday night, who was praying for me?" I didn't say anything, so she continued, "In the middle of that night, God woke me up and showed me I was heading toward the abyss, there was no bottom to it, I was scared to death, I was so frightened I realized how hard I'd been, how wrong, how rebellious, but at the same time it was like God wrapped his arms around me and held me tight, he kept me from sliding any further as he said, ' I still love you'." And I looked into her bloodshot eyes and once again I recognized the daughter we had raised.[39]

Our God is a good Father. He hears our prayers. Don't stop crying out. Always pray, and don't give up. Ask persistently, seek consistently, and knock with shameless audacity until the God of Heaven opens the door.

Read: Luke 18:1-8, Colossians 1:9-12, James 5:13-18

Reflect: Does "shameless audacity" describe my prayers?

Pray: Holy Spirit, thank You for interceding for me and teaching me to pray. Help me grow in faith and in prayer. Continue to teach me to ask, seek, and knock.

CHAPTER 34

REJOICE AND BE GLAD

Joy is not the absence of suffering but the presence of God.
—*Elisabeth Elliot*

In Matthew 5, Jesus begins the Sermon on the Mount with a familiar introduction called The Beatitudes or The Blessings. He stood in front of the crowd declaring: Blessed are the meek, the peacemakers, and the poor in spirit. Jesus's introduction was well thought out and Spirit-led. He was turning around our natural way of thinking about what it means to be blessed.

Do you remember the final blessing Jesus proclaimed here? It was a blessing that would give preface to the rest of His ministry. This final blessing is both joyful and tough:

> **"Blessed are those who are persecuted because of righteousness, for theirs is the kingdom of heaven. Blessed are you when people insult you, persecute you and falsely say all kinds of evil against you because of me. Rejoice and be glad because great is your reward in heaven, for in the same way they persecuted the prophets who were before you."**
> **Matthew 5:10-12**

Luke records Jesus's instruction this way: "Rejoice in that day and leap for joy" (Luke 6:23). We are literally commanded to be exceedingly glad and leap for joy. My (Todd's) mind immediately runs to kids at a trampoline park, jumping up and down. Can you picture that? Kids bouncing with exuberance, laughing, ecstatic. Or maybe what comes to your mind is a big, happy, noisy concert with people singing and jumping up and down to the beat of the band.

I think when Jesus said these words, He wanted His audience to picture King David in 2 Samuel 6. David, the young giant killer, is now the king of all Israel. For 20 years, the ark of the covenant had been kept in the private home of a man named Obed-Edom. But on this day, they brought the ark of the covenant back to Jerusalem with great pomp and circumstance. It was a parade, the streets lined with people. And this is what the Bible says about King David: He was wild in his rejoicing. Dancing before the Lord, David ripped his shirt off, leaping before the Lord with all his might.

Like King David, Jesus commands us to shout, leap, rejoice, and break into dancing, specifically when we are being persecuted, hated, and insulted. This may be among the most demanding of all Jesus's commands. It just doesn't seem to fit. I don't know about you, but it's not my first instinct to dance when somebody hurts me. It's not my initial response to rejoice and leap for joy when someone insults me. Instinctively, I want to yell, insult, and return the mean behavior.

However, blessings begin when we endure insults, slanders, and lies with joy because of Jesus. Let me remind you that we can rejoice in our trials because it is a sure thing that a reward is being banked up for us in Heaven. Rejoicing in trials helps us see beyond the present and remember that this life is short compared to eternity. Rejoicing in our trials is also the perfect antidote for hatred. When we alter our natural response with something supernatural, it helps us not to hate. When we rejoice in the face of peril and in the face of persecution, God moves. Sometimes we see it, and sometimes we don't, but we can be sure He is moving.

I wonder if when we arrive in Heaven and see all God has prepared for us, we will regret that we didn't sing more, rejoice more, or leap for joy more.

One of my favorite stories in the Bible is found in Acts 16. Paul and his partner Silas have traveled to Philippi as missionaries. They preached, performed miracles, and cast demons out of people. Because of their testimony about Jesus, they were lied about and arrested. The Romans stripped them naked and beat them within an inch of their life. Then they threw them into prison in solitary confinement, so to speak, with their arms and feet locked in stocks. One would think Paul and Silas would have felt abandoned in the dark and desperate place, but listen to how Luke describes their experience in Acts 16:25-26: "About midnight Paul and Silas were praying and singing hymns to God, and the other prisoners were listening to them. Suddenly there was such a violent earthquake that the foundations of the prison were shaken. At once all the prison doors flew open, and everyone's chains came loose."

The jailor on duty that night almost took his own life, thinking that all the prisoners had escaped. But after Paul showed him that everyone was accounted for, instead of suicide, the jailor became a believer in Jesus. He took Paul and Silas into his home, and his entire family was baptized by sunup! The church at Philippi was born.

I've often wondered what Paul and Silas were singing that night. We know it was a hymn. Maybe it was one of the Psalms of David. Perhaps even the words of Psalm 5 that seem to fit their situation:

> Lead me, Lord, in your righteousness because of my enemies—make your way straight before me. Not a word from their mouth can be trusted; their heart is filled with malice; their throat is an open grave; with their tongues they tell lies. Declare them guilty, O God! Let their intrigues be their downfall. Banish them for their many sins, for they have rebelled against you. But let all who take refuge in you be glad; let them ever sing for joy. Spread your protection over them that those who love your name may rejoice in you. Surely, Lord, you bless the righteous; you surround them with your favor as with a shield. (Psalm 5:8-12)

What song would you sing in the same situation as Paul and Silas? What words would be on your lips in hurt, pain, lies, deceit, exclusion, jail, and persecution? I know what song I'd sing: *It Is Well with My Soul*, a beautiful hymn of faith that helped many people get through trials. Part of the reason that song means so much to me is because of the story behind it.

In 1871 the author, Horatio Spafford, lost his fortune in the great fire of Chicago. Only a little time after that, his precious four-year-old little boy died of scarlet fever. In the family's loss and grief, they decided to take time away and go to England for respite.

Spafford sent his wife and four daughters ahead of him on the transatlantic journey by boat, planning to join them later. Tragically, their ship was involved in a terrible collision and sank. Two hundred people on board that vessel lost their lives, including all four of Horatio Spafford's daughters. His wife Anna managed to survive, and when she arrived in England, she telegraphed her husband, "Saved alone, what shall I do?"

Horatio Spafford got on a boat and set sail to join his grieving wife, himself overwhelmed by sorrow. Aware of his plight, the ship's captain called him to the bridge and took him out to the rail to show him where his family's boat had gone down. Looking over the rail, supernatural words of comfort washed over Spafford.[40]

Listen to these words of the now famous hymn: "When peace like a river attends my way, when sorrow like sea billows roll, whatever my lot, thou hast taught me to say, it is well with my soul. Though Satan should buffet, though trials should come let this blessed assurance control, that Christ has regarded my helpless estate and has shed his own blood for my soul. It is well."[41]

Friend, you may leave this world without ever being persecuted for your faith, but we have all experienced great trials of many kinds. Do you sing through them? I know that's tough. There are days when I need someone to remind me to rejoice as tragedy or sadness strikes me, when I need to get my perspective right and recognize that this world is not all there is. There's a better day coming.

When things get bad, when grief washes over you and me like breaking waves, when all seems lost, on the dark night, let's sing—*it is well with my soul*. All else may be lost, but our soul is intact, and great treasure has been laid up for us in Heaven, all because Jesus shed His blood for us.

Read: Romans 5:3-5 James 1:2-3, 1 Peter 1:6-9

Reflect: When hard times come, do I sing, dance, and leap for joy?

Pray: God, no matter what circumstances I face, I can say with confidence it is well with my soul. I choose to rejoice and sing with gratitude each and every day.

CHAPTER 35

REMEMBER ME

When Jesus wanted to explain to his disciples what his death was all about, he didn't give them a theory, he gave them a meal.
—*N.T. Wright*

One of Jesus's last commands to His disciples was in an upper room in Jerusalem. Jews from all around the world had gathered in Jerusalem to celebrate Passover. Knowing He would soon be betrayed, denied, arrested, and crucified, Jesus gathered His disciples to share in this Hebrew feast of remembrance.

Passover began in Egypt thousands of years earlier. The Hebrew people had been enslaved for nearly 400 years, suffering and crying out to God for deliverance. God heard their cries and sent Moses to Pharaoh with the demand, "Let God's people go, set them free." But Pharaoh refused. So, God brought a succession of awful plagues, including locusts, frogs, water to blood, flies, and darkness, and the final and worst plague of all, the death of the firstborn.

God sent a destroying angel to take the life of every firstborn son throughout Egypt, except in the land of Goshen, where the Hebrew slaves lived. Moses instructed the fathers there to take a young lamb without spot or blemish, kill it, set the body apart for a meal later that night, and take its blood and paint the doorpost of their home. Then, they were to gather their family inside behind that closed door covered with blood. As they watched and prayed that night, they hastily prepared a meal of unleavened bread, raw vegetables, boiled eggs, and Passover lamb. For centuries, Jewish people, scattered throughout the world, in an unbroken chain of years, even in times of holocaust or great distress, have celebrated Passover, remembering God's great deliverance on that very first Passover night.

When Jesus and His disciples gathered in the upper room to celebrate Passover, Jesus took the bread and the cup and inaugurated a brand-new historic *remembrance*—communion or the Lord's Supper. Paul records this moment:

> **"The Lord Jesus, on the night he was betrayed, took bread, and when he had given thanks, he broke it and said, 'This is my body, which is for you; do this in remembrance of me.' In the same way after supper, he took the cup saying, 'This cup is the new covenant in my blood, do this whenever you drink it and remember me.' For whenever you eat this bread and drink this cup, you proclaim the Lord's death until he comes."** I Corinthians 11:23-26

Jesus was declaring, "I am the Passover Lamb. It is My body, My blood." Remember when Jesus went to John the Baptist to be baptized, and John shouted out prophetically, "Behold, the Lamb of God, who takes away the sins of the world" (John 1:29 ESV). The Passover celebration is now altered. When we celebrate the Lord's Supper, the Christian church looks back, remembering the sacrifice of Jesus and looking forward to the day when He will come again.

Paul continues with instructions to the Corinthian church on how we should take communion: "So then, whoever eats the bread or drinks the cup of the Lord in an unworthy manner will be guilty of sinning against the body and blood of the Lord. Everyone ought to examine themselves before they eat of the bread and drink from the cup. For those who eat and drink without discerning the body of Christ eat and drink judgment on themselves" (I Corinthians 11:27-29).

I (Todd) struggled with these verses in my early Christian walk. Before taking the Lord's Supper, I would be reminded of all my sins of the week prior and would often skip communion out of fear. There were certain weeks, months, and even years that I didn't participate because I was scared that if I took communion unworthily, I could be eating and drinking condemnation and judgment on myself. Over my years in ministry, I have talked to many other believers who don't take communion because, based on this verse, they feel unworthy or frightened.

Let's clear up this misconception. In context, the church at Corinth was a wicked, carnal, fleshy church. They had all kinds of sin problems. One of their problems was they loved to party. Their worship services turned to chaos and a free-for-all. They turned the communion meal into a big drunken party, with overeating and overindulging. This is the "unworthy manner" Paul is talking about. His instructions are to remind the church that the communion meal is a time of sobriety and solemnness for us to remember the body and blood of Jesus.

Friend, let me be clear: Every time I take the Lord's Supper, I am unworthy, and so are you. But that's the point of the Lord's Supper: to remind us that in our lost sin condition, Jesus, the perfect Lamb of God, died for us as a sacrifice. During this time, we remember Him, acknowledge our unworthiness, examine ourselves, confess our sins, and embrace the Lord's forgiveness through His blood shed for us.

This simple meal of bread and wine has been shared among Christians for over two thousand years. Sometimes in a grass hut, sometimes underneath a tree, sometimes in a great cathedral with much pomp and ceremony. But it should always be accompanied by things sacred and solemn because, among other things, it is life-giving.

There's much for us to learn about this mysterious meal. Jesus taught His disciples about the Lord's Supper long before that night in the upper room. Early in His ministry, large crowds started following Jesus. They wanted to hear Him teach, they wanted to see Him perform miracles, and they brought their sick so that they could be healed. In John 6, by the Sea of Galilee, these crowds asked Jesus for a sign so they could believe. They wanted to see something physical, like the manna the Israelites received in the desert.

Jesus, in a very measured way, knowing what was coming, very purposely answered them by telling them that God the Father would give them true bread from Heaven. He explained, "I am the bread of life. Whoever comes to me will never go hungry, and whoever believes in me will never be thirsty" (John 6:35). The crowds started to grumble, wondering how this man who grew up nearby could claim to come from Heaven.

Jesus continued, "I am the living bread that came down from heaven. Whoever eats this bread will live forever. This bread is my flesh, which I will give for the life of the world. . . Unless you eat the flesh of the Son of Man and drink his blood, you have no life in you. Whoever eats my flesh and drinks my blood has eternal life and I will raise them up at the last day. For my flesh is real food and my blood is real drink" (John 6:51, 53-55).

Not surprisingly, a number of people following Jesus could not accept this hard teaching and turned away from following Him. Not only was

Jesus claiming to be God, but it sounded like He was preaching and teaching cannibalism—a great blasphemy to the Jews.

We know that Jesus didn't mean we have to literally eat His physical flesh and drink His blood to have eternal life. This teaching came full circle a few years later with His disciples there at the table in the upper room when He took the bread, broke it, and said, "This is my body which is broken for you" (I Corinthians 11:24 NKJV). I wonder if they thought back to His teaching recorded in John 6, "Oh, that's what he meant." And when He took the cup and blessed it and said, "This cup is the new covenant in my blood" (I Corinthians 11:26), they thought, "Oh, now I understand."

While the Lord's Supper is symbolic, I believe it is also sacramental. It is more than a tactile observance. A sacrament is a physical participation in the divine. When we share the Lord's Supper through these symbols, something supernatural takes place. I Corinthians 10:16 describes communion as participation in the blood and body of Christ. It is life to us. Martin Luther, the great reformer, wrote, 'To our eyes baptism appears to be nothing more than ordinary water, and the sacrament of Christ's body and blood simple bread and wine, like other bread and wine . . . But we must not trust what our eyes see."[42]

J.C. Ryle wrote this warning: "It is impossible to say that any professing Christian is in a safe, healthy, or satisfactory condition of soul, who habitually refuses to obey Christ and attend the Lord's table."[43] When we take the Lord's Supper, we step into something mysterious and divine. Let us never get to the point where it becomes routine, something we take in passing, simply checking a box.

Revelation 19 tells us there will be a great celebration in Heaven one day. The risen saints of all times will be invited to a banquet with Jesus at the head of the table. Jesus predicted this day in Matthew 26:29 when He said, "I tell you, I will not drink from this fruit of the vine from now on until that day when I drink it new with you in my Father's kingdom." We will celebrate eternally the wedding supper of the Lamb, remembering the great work of Christ and the sure and present resurrection.

Whenever you take communion, remember to look back and give thanks. Then look ahead and give thanks. Remembering Jesus as you participate in something . . . divine!

Remember Me

Read: Mark 14:22-25, Luke 22:14-20, Revelation 19:6-9

Reflect: What does communion mean to me?

Pray: Jesus, thank You for Your body broken and Your blood shed for me. Help me to remember Your sacrifice as I look forward to Your return.

SECTION 6

SHARING THE GOOD NEWS

But you will receive power when the Holy Spirit comes on you; and you will be my witnesses in Jerusalem, and in all Judea and Samaria, and to the ends of the earth.

Acts 1:8

CHAPTER 36

LET YOUR LIGHT SHINE

The demand that we let our light shine before the world has a goal. That people might give glory to our Father in Heaven. So, ultimately, the demand is that we seek to glorify God, we seek to glorify God by letting our light shine. Our light shines brightest and God is best glorified through our good deeds. —John Piper

In *The Merchant of Venice*, William Shakespeare wrote, "How far that little candle throws his beams! So shines a good deed in a weary world."[44] If you are unfamiliar with Shakespeare's works, maybe you're familiar with the song "This Little Light of Mine." Both Shakespeare's quote and this little children's song find their source in the Scripture, from Jesus's teaching in Matthew 5.

Remember how Jesus began the Sermon on the Mount with a list of those who are blessed? The humble, the meek, the pure in heart, those who are insulted and persecuted because of following Him? Jesus continues by saying:

> **"You are the salt of the earth. But if salt loses its saltiness, how can it be made salty again? It is no longer good for anything, except to be thrown out and trampled underfoot. You are the light of the world. A town built on a hill cannot be hidden. Neither do people light a lamp and put it under a bowl. Instead, they put it on its stand, and it gives light to everyone in the house. In the same way, let your light shine before others, that they may see your good deeds and glorify your Father in Heaven." Matthew 5:13-16**

Who is He talking to here? There's a great crowd there. Who are the "you's" of this passage? He is speaking to disciples of Christ throughout history. When Jesus says you are the salt of the earth, the light of the world, He is talking to us, His followers.

Let's talk about salt for a minute. Have you ever heard the phrase, "worth their salt"? Do you know where that came from? In antiquity, salt was a valued, highly prized commodity. In those days, it was a little more difficult to find, and Roman soldiers were paid in salt. It was called the *salarium*, and is where we get the word *salary* or this expression "worth your salt."[45]

Salt is an amazing mineral. Did you know our life is dependent on salt? Without it, we would die. Salt has many uses, including preserving, seasoning, melting ice, and pulling out impurities. Consider how this applies to us as Christians. We bring taste to a tasteless world through our words, service, and love. We are life preservers to a lost and dying world. We can provide soothing comfort, hope, and healing to hurting people. It's been through the work of the church, the salt of the world, that through the Gospel message, hard hearts have melted and given way to receive the love of Christ.

Let's go back to Matthew 5. Jesus states we are the salt and light of the world, and then He gives one of His first commands: let your light shine through your good deeds, and the world will take notice and glorify God.

Often, we confuse Jesus's command and think of a church on a hill with all the lights on and everybody inside, singing and praising God with people down in the valley listening. That's not what Jesus says. Instead, He teaches that, like a clearly visible city on a hill, the light of our *good deeds* cannot be hidden. We shine our light when we do good to others. We glorify God, and we help unbelievers glorify God when we live salty and brilliant lives in service to others.

In the 1500s, William Tyndale, a great man of God, took it upon himself to begin translating the Word of God into common English so every man could read and understand it. The church fathers in that day did not allow the common person to read the Scriptures or even have a copy of them. Tyndale's mission was not only rejected by the church, but he was branded a heretic. They hunted William Tyndale all over Europe. Finally catching up to him, they strangled him to death and burned his body at the stake. But even in that dark time, William Tyndale made this observation about the church, "The church is the one institution that exists for those outside it."[46]

What's the purpose of the church and our gathering together each week? So that we can leave, salty and shining! The church is the place where we prepare ourselves for real ministry to outsiders.

It's not hard. It doesn't take much to be the salt of the earth, really. It doesn't take much to leave a good taste in the heart and mind of someone lost in darkness. Doesn't take much, just a candle shooting its beam into the darkness. Listen to what Jesus said in Matthew 10:22: "If anyone gives a cup of cold water to one of these little ones, I tell you the truth, that person will certainly not lose their reward."

A cup of cold water, given in the name of Jesus, given out of mercy, blesses a child, blesses the thirsty, blesses those hurting and suffering. In small ways and in great ways, we can be salt and light to the world, and they will glorify the Father in Heaven.

Recently, when I (Todd) was on my phone, browsing around, I came across this expression of gratitude that summarizes this lesson so well: "If you were the lunch lady in a small public elementary school in East Orange, New Jersey, in the early 80s and you snuck a small, shy girl with blue eyes and bangs a peanut butter sandwich on the days she had no lunch money, know that I have loved you my entire life and hope you've been happy and healthy."[47]

The smallest acts, done from a kind heart, make profound differences in people's lives.

Read: Colossians 3:17, Colossians 4:5-6, I Timothy 6:17-19, Hebrews 10:23-25

Reflect: How am I sharing God's light? What good deeds can I do that will help other people see God?

Pray: God, help Your church to be salty. Let us season, preserve, and melt hard hearts. Open my eyes to see the opportunities, big or small, to shine Your light and love today.

CHAPTER 37

INVITE THE POOR

When a poor person dies of hunger, it has not happened because God did not take care of him or her. It has happened because neither you nor I wanted to give that person what he or she needed.
—*Mother Teresa*

Have you driven up to an intersection, and there, standing in the grass, is a man or woman holding up a little cardboard sign? If you are like me (Stacey), questions begin to race through your mind. We can do so many different things at that moment, but what does God expect? As followers of Jesus, we are called to love the world and to love our neighbors, and there they are with a sign, "Veteran, please help" or "Need food, will work."

You might think that, as a pastor, I should know what to do. After all, I am paid to reach out and love people. You might assume that when I drive up to those intersections, I get out of the car, hand them my keys, and give them everything in my wallet. But if I can be honest, sometimes I start to pray the light turns green so I can keep moving. Sometimes, I give out a bag of snacks and water bottles, a gift card for food, or even a New Testament. But sometimes, I only helped because my children were in the back seat asking, "What are we going to do for that man, Daddy?"

Listen, I've tried it all. I've literally taken those men on the side of the road and brought them to my house and put them to work. But the longer I work at this, the less sure I am of how to handle these situations. In over twenty years in professional ministry, working in this arena has clarified some things and made some more confusing. The only thing I know for sure is that knowing what we should do and how we should respond to the poor and needy takes tremendous discernment, prayer, love, and way all too often, an investment of time.

As Jesus's ministry started to take off and gain momentum, He took His little band of disciples and anyone else willing to follow, and they literally ping-ponged all over that Galilean countryside. They were not in any one spot for more than a few days. As Christ's popularity grew, He became a superstar. It was a huge deal to show up in the community where Jesus was.

In the evenings, Jesus and His disciples would visit various homes. Can you imagine the excitement if Jesus ended up in your home? People from all over the community would have poured through any door or window they could get to. Imagine how privileged the seats at your dinner table would become. It is like when you serve cake at a kid's birthday party, and all the kids are pushing and elbowing to be at the front of the line.

In Luke 14, Jesus had dinner at the house of a local religious leader. As grown adults elbowed to get the best seats, Jesus reprimanded them for their self-centered and self-promoting attitude. Then, He turned to the owner of the house, a leader among the Pharisees, and said:

> **"When you give a luncheon or dinner, do not invite your friends, your brothers or sisters, your relatives, or your rich neighbors; if you do, they may invite you back and so you will be repaid. But when you give a banquet, invite the poor, the crippled, the lame, the blind, and you will be blessed. Although they cannot repay you, you will be repaid at the resurrection of the righteous."**   Luke 14:12-14

There must have been a lot of sheepish, embarrassed looks, people avoiding Jesus's gaze as He gave them these humbling instructions. I'm sure the host of the party must have felt some level of betrayal as his dinner guest called him out in front of his peers. After all, the man had only done what most of us would have done, inviting those closest to him to his dinner party.

This concept of giving attention to the poor, crippled, lame, and blind was not new. Jesus had often taught His followers to give to the poor at their own expense. Like the rich young man whom Jesus told to sell everything he had and give it to the poor so he could have treasure in Heaven. Or when Jesus said in Luke 12:33, "Sell your possessions and give to the poor. Provide purses for yourselves that will not wear out." Jesus is clear: God values the downtrodden and expects us to do the same.

But what exactly does it mean to invite the poor to dinner, especially if we've already sent out the invitations to our next dinner party? As we

Invite the Poor

work to fully comprehend Jesus's instruction here, I want to draw from the greater context of the Bible. We are going to look at three Scriptures that help us properly understand this challenging command.

The first is written by the Apostle Paul. II Thessalonians 3:10 says, "The one who is unwilling to work shall not eat." This may seem like a strange place to start our study on what it means to begin inviting the disadvantaged to our table. On the surface, this statement seems like it belongs nailed over the door of some mess hall of an army barracks or a military school, though some of you with teenagers may want to frame it to hang over your refrigerator. But seriously, what do we do with this straightforward advice?

While at a glance, it seems to contradict Jesus's teaching to love our neighbors as ourselves, keep in mind this is not an Old Testament word given by Moses but instead written to the New Testament church. I believe this simple instruction begins to bring some balance to how we are supposed to interact with the poor. Friends, it's so important that we make a distinction between those who are truly needy and those who are needy due to their own lack of self-discipline, lack of effort, or even their appetite for sin.

Paul would continue in II Thessalonians 3:11-12 NLT: "Yet we hear that some of you are living idle lives, refusing to work and meddling in other people's business. We command such people and urge them in the name of the Lord Jesus Christ to settle down and work to earn their own living." Paul was clearly not referring to people who truly could not work due to either debilitating physical handicaps, severe illness, or even the limitations of old age. Think of how Jesus spelled out who would qualify for an invitation to the dinner party: poor, lame, crippled, and blind. By and large, these words describe people with limitations entirely outside of their control. The Bible clearly expects that you should provide for yourself if it is within your power.

After years of outreach in our local community, our church's outreach team has realized that there is a balance to be struck between helping those who are incapable of helping themselves and helping those who simply won't help themselves. Picture this scene: Little Jimmy is acting out, and his parents are about to lose their minds. He's yelling and pulling candy off the shelf despite being told to put it back. His mom finally says, "Listen, I'll buy you some candy if you'll just stop." Friends, if you've ever seen that happen (or been that mom or dad), you know what enabling is. The devastating habit of enabling or rewarding bad and destructive behaviors is one of the most unloving things we can ever do. And it doesn't stop at childhood or with our children; it continues right into adulthood and works into our day-to-day lives.

We all received great undeserved kindness when we became followers of Jesus, and we believe every person is eligible for some measure of undeserved kindness. But friends, that undeserved kindness needs to be measured carefully, or we could be aiding in a sinful man or woman's ultimate destruction. There's so much more I could share in this area, but I think it's sufficient to say that I don't believe that Jesus's command to bring in the needy is some broad-brush approach that we should apply to people without some tremendous prayer and discernment.

Now let's look at the second verse, Proverbs 19:17: "If you help the poor, you are lending to the LORD—and he will repay you." In some supernatural way that I will never fully understand, what we do for the genuinely poor and needy is felt and received by God Himself. Any time you have given to a person who genuinely needed it, somehow God felt that, accepted it, and appreciated it. It's an amazing thing to consider. It's like Jesus said in Matthew 25:40, "I tell you the truth, when you did it to one of the least of these my brothers and sisters, you were doing it to me!" When we take care of the poor, visit the prisoners, and feed the hungry, we are caring for Jesus. Charity and acts of kindness done out of love for Christ have a ripple effect that is felt right through the physical realm and into the throne room of God Himself.

Hang on to that thought as we look at the final verse, Revelation 3:17: "You say, 'I am rich; I have everything I want. I don't need a thing!' But you don't realize that you are wretched and miserable and poor and blind and naked." Jesus is speaking to the church here; this statement is made to believers. Notice that this person claims, "I'm rich; I don't need a thing," only to be corrected by the Lord that they are, in fact, wretched and miserable. Jesus's gaze sees right through the outward appearance, the persona we put on, and pierces right to our hearts. What He finds when He peers inside of that spiritual place determines whether you are truly wealthy or poor.

Do you remember where you were when Jesus found you and invited you to sit at His table? Before He rescued us, we were more helpless and needy than the homeless man on the street corner with the cardboard sign. We had nothing to offer, nothing to pay our way into that place of great honor, seated with Jesus Christ. We were undeserving, broken, and filled with sin. And the price of entry wasn't a crumpled five-dollar bill, an inexpensive Bible, or a bottle of water that we've given away at the street corner. Our entrance was paid by the precious blood of Jesus Christ. It is because God has treated you and me this way that we are expected, even commanded, to share that same generous love with the downtrodden in our own lives.

Read: Psalm 40:17, Isaiah 58:6-8, James 2:1-17

Reflect: How does remembering where I was when Christ found me impact how I see the poor and needy?

Pray: Jesus, thank You for inviting me to sit at Your table. Help me to extend that same grace and love to others. Teach me how to show compassion and help the poor and needy in my community.

CHAPTER 38

LET THE CHILDREN COME

We live in an age when a thousand seductive voices beckon for the ears and the minds of our children. It is not enough to teach them a few rote prayers. Our homes must be so filled with the presence of Jesus that they encounter him at every turn, come to know him and love him as effortlessly as they come to know their parents and in such a setting Jesus can engage their loyalty and fire their imagination and this is the only antidote to the powers of darkness and corruption which are loose in the world today. —Larry Christianson

The Gospel of Mark paints a picture of a day when large crowds of people were following Jesus, hundreds and maybe even thousands. And everyone wanted something from Jesus—to be touched, to be healed, to hear a word. The scene is loud and chaotic. People were rushing, pushing, fighting to get to the front of the line. The disciples were working security and crowd control, and we can imagine they were hot, anxious, nervous, and most likely frustrated. Maybe as they held back the long line, they would shout, "Get back, wait your turn, stay in line, quit yelling!"

In the midst of this craziness, moms and dads are bringing their children to Jesus for His blessing. Can you see them rushing forward, holding up their babies to the Lord so they can be touched by the Master? Listen to how Mark describes the scene:

> **"People were bringing little children to Jesus for him to place his hands on them, but the disciples rebuked them. When Jesus saw this, he was indignant. He said to them, 'Let the little children come to me, and do not hinder them, for the kingdom of God belongs to such as these. Truly I tell you, anyone who will not receive the kingdom of God like a little child will never enter it.'"** Mark 10:13-16

Jesus not only welcomes children, He commands His followers, "Let the children come to me." As parents, teachers, grandparents, and church family, all of us together need to ask ourselves the question: Are we eagerly and obediently bringing our children to Jesus? We are all responsible for making a way for children to come— introducing them to Jesus, giving them access, letting them engage their faith and curiosity, and allowing them to encounter Jesus and receive His blessing.

Notice Jesus's command to "let the little children come" also includes the warning: "Do not hinder them." We need to examine ourselves to find out if we are hindering or restraining children's access to Jesus. Holding children back from Jesus is often not intentional. It happens out of neglect, out of apathy, or out of just not thinking about it.

Most parents are serious about ensuring their children have the best education, receive proper health care, learn how to work well with others, and develop skills and talents. They know raising children is an investment; it's expensive, and it takes a lot of time, energy, and effort. But often, parents don't invest the same effort in their children's spiritual well-being as they do toward their physical well-being. They don't take seriously Jesus's command to introduce their children to Jesus, to be on the frontline of training them to love and obey Him.

Voddie Baucham said, "Disciplining our children is not about teaching them to behave in a way that won't embarrass us. We're working toward something much more important than that. We're actually raising our children with a view toward leading them to trust and to follow Christ."[48]

Centuries before Jesus walked the earth, interacting with these very parents and children, God gave instructions for how to teach children to follow Him. "Fix these words of mine in your hearts and minds. Tie them as symbols on your hands, bind them on your foreheads. Teach them to your children, talking about them when you sit at home, when you walk along the road, when you lie down, when you get up. Write them on the doorframes of your houses and on your gates" (Deuteronomy 11:18-20).

Frederick Douglass is quoted saying, "It is easier to build strong children than to repair broken men." In his biography, Douglass shares how he learned about Jesus in an unconventional way — by eavesdropping near an open window as his master's wife would read the Bible to her children. Both of his parents died when Frederick was only six years old. As a child, he slept on a dirt floor, scrounged for food, and had no schooling. He taught himself to read and write from a Webster's spelling book and posters.[49]

At age 13, Douglass gave his life to Christ. He later escaped slavery and went on to become one of the most influential people in American history, leading the abolitionist movement and becoming a Presidential Elector, United States Marshal, United States Recorder, and United States diplomat.

Because he had become a Christian, this great man of God, who had escaped both physical and spiritual slavery, forgave his abusive former master. In September of 1848, on the 10th anniversary of his escape, Douglass published an open letter addressed to his former master, a man named Thomas Auld, berating him for his conduct. Saying, "Oh sir, a slave holder never appears to me so completely an agent of hell, as when I think of and look upon my own dear children. It is then that my feelings rise above my control. The grim horrors of slavery rise in all their ghastly terror before me. The wails of millions pierce my heart and chill my blood."[50]

In the New Testament, the Apostle Paul likens sin to slavery. He depicts our old lives without Christ as a form of captivity. We were held in chains by a strict master, Satan. But when Jesus came into our lives, those chains were broken, the doors were open, and slaves were set free. Satan's intention is to capture our children, enslave them in his grip, and hold them in the bonds and chains of sin so that they will do his will. Children are surrounded by relentless voices urging them at every turn, every click, to turn from their faith in Jesus.

In Mark 9:42, Jesus says, "If anyone causes one of these little ones-those who believe in me to stumble, it would be better for them if a large millstone were hung around their neck, and they were thrown into the sea." In the original language, the word *stumble* in Greek is the word *skandalon*. That word literally means a tripwire, like making a trap to ensnare an animal in. There are wicked people with a Satanic agenda, setting traps right now for our children. Trip wires along their path, enticing them, seducing them away from Jesus. We need to stand against them. We need to be hyper-aware and hyper-vigilant to rescue our children from those snares. We must bring our children to Jesus.

When you think about Satan's plan for children, does it pierce your heart? Do your feelings "rise above your control"? We must all work together, standing shoulder to shoulder, to deliver our children from Satan's deceit and into the freedom that Jesus provides.

Frederick Douglass began his path of following Jesus through overhearing a mother reading Scripture to her children. A child hungry, destitute, absolutely alone, at the mercy of the wicked hand of the slave owner, yet he comes to Jesus by overhearing bedtime stories. That's the power of the Word. Let me ask you, parents, are your children hearing it? Straight forward, plain and clear from you? Are you leading your children to Jesus?

Read: Proverbs 22:6, Matthew 18:1-5, 2 Timothy 2:25, I Peter 5:8

Reflect: Am I actively helping children come to Jesus? Am I doing anything that might hinder children from coming to Jesus?

Pray: God, I pray for the children in my home, my church, and my community. Protect them from the lies of the enemy. Help them find the freedom Jesus offers them. Raise up a generation that seeks You.

CHAPTER 39

DO NOT JUDGE

The Holy Bible is like a mirror. A mirror before our mind's eye. In it we see our inner face. From the Scriptures we learn our spiritual deformities and beauty and thereto we discover the progress we are making and how far we are from perfection.
—*Pope Gregory the First*

I (Stacey) have always enjoyed the story told by Pastor Henry Ironside about a man named Bishop Potter. Potter was sailing for Europe on one of the great transatlantic ocean liners. Once on board, he found that another passenger was sharing his cabin. He went to the concierge's desk and inquired if he could leave his gold watch and other valuables in the ship's safe. He explained that ordinarily, he would never avail himself of that privilege, but he had been to his cabin and met the man who would occupy the room with him. Judging from the man's appearance, he was afraid he would not be a very trustworthy person. The concierge accepted the valuables and remarked, "It's all right, Bishop; I'll be very glad to take care of them for you. The other man has already been here and has left his for the same reason."[51]

Let's look again to the Sermon on the Mount. My guess is when Jesus shared this command about judging others, it universally connected and was felt across the crowd:

> **"Do not judge, or you too will be judged. For in the same way you judge others, you will be judged, and with the same measure you use, it will be measured to you."**
> **Matthew 7:1-2**

Over the years, the church has received many labels. Of all the labels given, there haven't been many that have stuck as effectively as "judgmental." You don't have to have lived long to have heard somebody say,

"Don't judge me." This demand may have different meanings to different people, but I think it's fair to say that for most, it simply means *don't look at my life and make negative assumptions about who I am based on what I'm doing, what I look like, or what I'm saying. Just accept me for who I am.*

This request for blanket acceptance, regardless of what you're doing, is nothing new. In many ways, this open acceptance can be very Christlike. At Bridge Christian Church, we offer everyone the invitation to "come as you are." However, that is only half of the invitation; the other half is "don't stay as you are." And this is where things start to get messy. As the church holds to this standard and expects its members to do the same, the label of being judgmental is sure to follow.

Unfortunately, this isn't the only reason the church has earned this label. Far too often, Jesus's followers have stepped far beyond gentle and loving accountability and moved to condemnation and finger-pointing. Instead of reconciliation and love, we've reached into the lives of people with a hammer, trying to bring about change instead of extending Christlike love.

The Bible is a powerful tool at our disposal as we speak into the lives of others. There are things you can speak as a believer in Jesus that can only be described as absolute truth. We're armed with something that can bring both salvation and, oddly enough, great harm.

When we read the Bible, a natural humility and thankfulness should come over our hearts as we realize how lost and sinful we were when Christ found us. Like a mirror, the Bible is a powerful reflector of our innermost being, daily reminding us of our constant need for Jesus. As we see our sinful hearts reflected on its pages, we should be drawn to our Savior's feet. However, if we are not careful, as we grow in understanding and knowledge, a subtle transition can take place in our hearts.

The more righteous and the more religious I think I am, the less I see my face in the mirror of Scripture, but instead, I begin to see only yours. All of a sudden, the sermons that I hear are no longer for me but for my spouse. The Scriptures I read fail to point out the sins hiding in me; instead, they only highlight the evil I see in you. In a slow, methodical transition, I no longer see my own depravity; I see only yours. It is a perilous situation when we are armed with God's truth but no longer apply it to ourselves.

While we should celebrate our salvation and the work God is doing in us, we cannot forget the reality of our sinfulness. Throughout the Bible,

God continues to balance His wonderful reminders of forgiveness with the reality that for the here and now, we are deeply sinful and prone to wandering. In I Timothy 1:15, listen to how Paul describes himself: "This is a trustworthy saying, and everyone should accept it: 'Christ Jesus came into the world to save sinners—and I am the worst of them all.'" Notice Paul doesn't use some past tense here—I was the worst of them all before I came to Christ. No, the writer of much of our New Testament is admitting openly and publicly that today, as I work out my salvation, I am the worst of them all.

I'm not sure there's a more dangerous thing than a church filled with red-faced Christians pounding their fists down on their self-righteous pulpits, judging, with unvarnished truth, the lives of lost people. Jesus illustrates this in a powerful parable found in Luke 18. Two men went to the Temple to pray. One was a Pharisee who prayed, thanking God he was not like other sinful people. He boasted of fasting and tithing. The second was a tax collector who stood off to the side with his eyes lowered, asking God for mercy because he was a sinner. Jesus explained, "I tell you, this sinner, not the Pharisee, returned home justified before God. For those who exalt themselves will be humbled, and those who humble themselves will be exalted" (Luke 18:14 NLT).

Imagine how shocked this puffed up and prideful religious man would be to find out that it's the humble tax collector and sinner, not himself, who will walk away justified before God. You and I would be wise to periodically ask ourselves the question, "Who am I seeing in the mirror of God's Word?" Are you seeing yourself, your sin, or only the shortcomings of others?

In Matthew 7, when Jesus commanded, "Do not judge others," the Greek word that He used for *judge* means *to distinguish, to decide, to condemn, or to punish*.[52] The word carries a sense of finality and decisiveness. The verdict from the person passing judgment on someone else is intended to be both piercing and unalterable. The problem with human beings communicating such grave and eternal indictment on another person is that you and I only see the exterior. But only one can see through the outward facade and into the heart of man, and that is God Himself.

We're reminded in I Samuel 16:7 NLT: "The Lord doesn't see things the way you see them. People judge by outward appearance, but the Lord looks at the heart." Not only does God see the heart of the person, but He also sees their future, who they will become. We must remember that the only heart we can see, the only heart we can begin to know, is our own. We remain humble by looking inwardly at our own hearts, aware of our sins, inabilities, and shortcomings. Ironically enough, in this place of being prostrated before God in humility, we are given the task of carefully, lovingly, and wisely exercising Biblical Christ-like judgment.

Jesus continued His lesson on judgment with these wise words: "And why worry about a speck in your friend's eye when you have a log in your own? How can you think of saying to your friend, 'Let me help you get rid of that speck in your eye', when you can't see past the log in your own. Hypocrite! First get rid of the log in your own eye; then you will see well enough to deal with the speck in your friend's eye" (Matthew 7:3-5). Notice there is room to confront others, but only after you've dealt with your own sin issues.

There are times as Christians when we are called to speak truth, even judgment, into the lives of other believers. We do it for the benefit of both the person who has wandered off the path and the church body. The Apostle Paul illustrates this very well in I Corinthians as he shares a true-life experience that happened in the church in Corinth and could occur in any church today.

> I can hardly believe the report about the sexual immorality going on among you—something that even pagans don't do. I am told that a man in your church is living in sin with his stepmother. You are so proud of yourselves, but you should be mourning in sorrow and shame. And you should remove this man from your fellowship. Even though I am not with you in person, I am with you in the Spirit. And as though I were there, I have already passed judgment on this man in the name of the Lord Jesus. You must call a meeting of the church. I will be present with you in spirit, and so will the power of our Lord Jesus. Then you must throw this man out and hand him over to Satan so that his sinful nature will be destroyed and he himself will be saved on the day the Lord returns. Your boasting about this is terrible. Don't you realize that his sin is like a little yeast that spreads through the whole batch of dough? (I Corinthians 5:1-6)

When we read this account carefully, we see two things happening. First, we see Paul's judgment on the sinful man, with the aim and hope that he will be restored by going through a season of hardship in the world. Second, we see Paul's desire to protect the church from a sin that can spread throughout the entire church if it is not addressed.

I can't stress enough the importance of humility, prayer, and good counsel when confronting sin in the lives of hurting people. Again, it's critical that you and I continually take inventory of our lives, so we don't fall prey to the very things Jesus warns us about. But we also need to take seriously our responsibility to lovingly share truth with others.

One day, our Lord will return from Heaven in a blink of an eye. In that moment, those who have not placed their faith in Jesus Christ and obeyed His commands will be judged, resulting in condemnation. But Jesus already made a way to avoid that judgment by paying the price for our sins. You and I are commissioned to share that message of both warning and reconciliation with the world.

But friends, how can we share it if we are living in the very same way that they are, if our lives are indistinguishable from people who don't set foot in a church? If we are going to unstick the judgmental label from our backs, we have to start living like Jesus and obeying His commands. Then, in the humbleness of our hearts with the same attitude that Jesus had when hordes of unbelievers crowded in to hear His message, we can share the Gospel in our workplaces, homes, and schools.

Read: Matthew 18:15-20, Philippians 2:12, Romans 2:1-3, James 1:22-25

Reflect: Who am I seeing in the mirror of God's Word today?

Pray: Jesus, forgive me for the times when I spend more time pointing my finger at other people than I do looking at my own shortcomings. Help me not to judge, but also teach me to lovingly speak truth into the lives of others.

CHAPTER 40

GO THE SECOND MILE

When people's lives please the LORD, even their enemies are at peace with them.
—King Solomon

We've all heard stories about a person who, in a moment that was critical to someone else's life, did something heroic. They didn't have time to react; they only had time to selflessly give themselves to a situation, and it's amazing. Have you wondered how you would respond in the same situation?

I (Stacey) read one such story recently about a man named Julio Diaz. One night, Diaz, a 31-year-old social worker, ended his hour-long subway ride in New York City one stop early to visit his favorite diner. Diaz stepped off the train onto a near-empty platform when his evening took an unexpected turn. As he walked toward the stairs, a teenage boy approached and pulled out a knife, demanding Diaz's money. Diaz gave him his wallet, but as the teen walked away, Diaz said, "Hey, wait a minute, you're forgetting something; if you're going to be robbing people the rest of the night, you might as well take my coat to keep you warm." Confused, the young robber looked at his generous victim, "What's going on here? Why are you doing this?" Diaz replied, "If you are willing to risk your freedom for just a few dollars, then I guess you must really need the money."

Then, Diaz did something even more unexpected; he asked the teen to join him for dinner. Amazingly, the two left what should have been a crime scene and went to dinner together. Later, when the bill arrived, Diaz said, "Look, you are going to have to pay for this bill because you have all my money; however, if you'd be willing to give me my wallet back, I'd gladly treat you." Without even thinking about it, the teen returned the wallet. As they departed, Diaz offered the boy twenty dollars in exchange for his knife. The boy willingly made the trade and walked off into the night.[53]

What an unexpected response to evil intentions. If I am honest, that is most likely not how the story would have played out if I was in Diaz's place. My response to evil is often so unlike what Jesus is calling us to. Listen to His words:

> "You have heard that it was said, 'Eye for eye, and tooth for tooth.' But I tell you, do not resist an evil person. If anyone slaps you on the right cheek, turn to them the other cheek also. And if anyone wants to sue you and take your shirt, hand over your coat as well. If anyone forces you to go one mile, go with them two miles. Give to the one who asks you, and do not turn away from the one who wants to borrow from you." Matthew 5:38-42

The Bible records moments throughout Jesus's ministry when He shared difficult truths, and people would leave, literally walking off in disbelief. I wonder if this was one of those times when some of his audience finally muttered, "I'm out." Thinking *this is too much, this is too hard. Don't resist an evil person? Offer your other cheek, your coat, go an extra mile?* Even for the faithful followers of Christ, this can feel like too much to expect. However, this is exactly what He commanded.

Later, the Apostle Paul would echo this teaching to the Roman church, "Dear friends, never take revenge. Leave that to the righteous anger of God. For the Scriptures say, 'I will take revenge; I will pay them back,' says the Lord. Instead, 'If your enemies are hungry, feed them. If they are thirsty, give them something to drink. In doing this, you will heap burning coals of shame on their heads. Don't let evil conquer you, but conquer evil by doing good'" (Romans 12:19-21).

If we want to truly understand the why behind Jesus's command not to resist an evil person, I believe it may boil down to that single statement, "Don't let evil conquer you, but conquer evil by doing good." Let's be honest: It's not our natural response to treat our enemies with kindness. Unless, of course, we're thinking of the phrase, "kill them with kindness." That approach seems okay since, at the end of our kindness, our enemies are dead. I feel a lot better about showing kindness if my kindness will make my enemies feel terrible about themselves or even destroy them.

As an American, I live in a nation that provides the right to bear arms, a country that has fought great wars and defeated our enemies on the field of battle. The United States, which I am so proud to be a part of, has long been a force for good in the world and, to this day, helps to fight the wars of other people across the globe. However, it is important to note that there is a God-given distinction between how our government handles its enemies and how the followers of Jesus handle theirs.

When it comes to punishing and deterring evil, God has given a special authority to our governing officials. In Romans 13, Paul reminds us that we should submit ourselves to those governing authorities because God has established them. "For the one in authority is God's servant for your good. But if you do wrong, be afraid, for rulers do not bear the sword for no reason. They are God's servants, agents of wrath to bring punishment on the wrongdoer" (Romans 13:4).

You might be wondering what this sidetrack about the government has to do with loving our enemies. But, I think, in all actuality, it becomes a significant reassurance as we carry out Jesus's command to resist the evil person. Not only has God instituted powerful governing authorities to handle the evil people in this world, but He will also act on His own accord. Remember, vengeance is God's. We can respond confidently to our enemies with undeserved grace, even kindness, knowing that our Heavenly Father does not forget our suffering at the hands of others.

It is easy to hear Jesus's words and go to extreme cases like someone breaking into our home, hurting our family, pulling a gun, etc. But every single day, there are hundreds of smaller, less significant times that we interact with our enemies. Most of us need to be more concerned about how we react to being cut off in traffic, when coworkers borrow our stapler and don't return it or eat our food in the office fridge, or when that family member writes cruel things on social media, friends that talk about us behind our back, bosses that ask unreasonable things of us, or even children that can at times act more like enemies than family. Jesus is not only addressing the extreme cases of evil, but His command invades my daily interactions and behaviors.

Whether the infraction against us is large or small, we have the assurance that if we treat our enemies with kindness, the Lord will bring a reckoning. But before you start thinking, *Great, God will smite them at some point in His perfect timing with fire from Heaven*, remember the words of Numbers 14:18 NLT: "The Lord is slow to anger and filled with unfailing love, forgiving every kind of sin and rebellion." Suppose we truly find it within ourselves to offer our enemies kindness and blessing in return for their evil, all the while expecting God to take immediate action on our behalf. There's a possibility we could be very disappointed.

The story of Jonah shows how this type of situation plays out in real-time. Jonah was a prophet of God. God called him to go to the city of Nineveh and preach, telling them they needed to repent or they would be destroyed. So, Jonah headed down to the docks and got on a ship going in precisely the opposite direction. He hated the Ninevites. They were wicked and evil, and Jonah didn't want to warn them; he wanted them to suffer. But as he tried to escape from the will of God, a storm came up, and Jonah ended up being cast overboard to save the ship. Jonah was swallowed by a great fish and then, three days later, found himself being spit out on the shores of Nineveh. Begrudgingly, mumbling to himself, he walked through that city and gave anyone who would listen the warning of God.

Next is the part that most children's books leave out. Jonah went up to a high place over the city and settled in to watch how that city would burn as these people finally got what they had coming. But instead, the Bible tells us something amazing happened. From the King of Nineveh to the lowest slave, the entire city put on sackcloth and ashes and wept in repentance for what they had done. As Jonah sat on that hill expecting condemnation and fire from Heaven, the Bible records that he felt great displeasure and misery when he learned that the great city had repented and would be spared from destruction. Despite Jonah's resistance, God showed undeserved kindness and grace in response to evil.

Friends, we need to brace ourselves for the possibility that when we leave the revenge to God, He may respond to those who hurt us with kindness and mercy. I think we are given a glimpse of why God responds to sinners with undeserved kindness in Romans 2:4 NLT: "Don't you see how wonderfully kind, tolerant, and patient God is with you? Does this mean nothing to you? Can't you see that his kindness is intended to turn you from your sin?"

The longer I study Jesus's commands, the more I see certain themes emerge. One of those may be best expressed by Walt Kelley's quote in a cartoon from the 1960s, in which he made this simple one-sentence assertion: "We have met the enemy, and he is us."[54] Friends, whenever I point my finger in condemnation at some evil, brokenness, or wickedness in our society, God turns the mirror reflection on me. We have been extended undeserved and unmerited kindness as enemies of God. His eyes looked into your future and saw the person you had become. Instead of judgment and condemnation, He gave you grace and adoption.

And now Jesus is calling us to love our enemies as He loved us. Like Jonah, we have the opportunity to share the Good News of God's mercy with those in desperate need, those who are far from God. With this undeserved kindness—turning the other cheek, giving away our possessions, and going the extra mile—we display God's love and forgiveness.

Read: Romans 5:6-11, Ephesians 4:31-32, I Peter 3:8-12

Reflect: Where do I have an opportunity to show undeserved kindness today?

Pray: Jesus, thank You for challenging me to love in a way that makes me depend on You. I cannot show kindness to my enemies without Your Holy Spirit transforming me. Help me to continue to learn to see others with Your eyes.

CHAPTER 41

LOVE YOUR ENEMIES

You never so touch the ocean of God's love as when you forgive your enemies.   —Corrie ten Boom

If you look at Jesus's commands, most can be divided into two main categories. Jesus would say things, and even His own disciples would pull Him aside and say, "Okay, what did you mean by that? That doesn't make any sense." But then there were these other times when Jesus said something so clear, so black and white, there was no way it could mean anything else. It was just really hard to do.

As we look again to the Sermon on the Mount, we find one of those commands that might leave you saying, "I understand what you're saying, Jesus, but that's not possible; I can't do that." We've already looked at how Jesus calls us to show undeserved kindness to our enemies, but now He takes it even further:

> **"You have heard that it was said, 'Love your neighbor and hate your enemy.' But I tell you, love your enemies and pray for those who persecute you."** Matthew 5:43-44

It's worth mentioning that the Greek language this Scripture was written in contains at least five words for love. In English, we say we love our wife, and we love our pizza, but in Greek, different words are used. Of all the Greek words for love, *agape* is the highest order, the most powerful. It's *agape* love we see in John 3:16: "For God so loved (*agape*) the world that he gave his one and only Son, that whoever believes in him shall not perish but have eternal life." This word for love describes care and compassion that are unconditional, unearned, and given, whether deserved or not.[55] We might assume that Jesus would have used some lesser Greek word regarding our love for our enemies, but that is not true. Jesus also uses *agape* to inform the type of love we should have for those who hate us.

Listen again as Jesus makes this command with a little more detail in Luke 6:35: "But love your enemies, do good to them, and lend to them without expecting to get anything back. Then your reward will be great, and you will be children of the Most High, because he is kind to the ungrateful and wicked." It would have been easier if Jesus had kept this command generic. But Jesus gives us real details on how to carry it out, which honestly makes me (Stacey) uncomfortable. Let's look at how Jesus defines loving your enemy.

First, He says to pray for those who persecute you. I don't know about you, but my first thought is *I so often fail to pray for the people that I love on a daily basis, and now I also need to pray for my enemies. Do you mean on the same list where I write down the names of people I genuinely care about who have cancer, are struggling with children, or need new employment, I'm supposed to create a little section in there for my enemies?*

And how do we begin to pray for the people who make our lives so difficult? Maybe you think you figured out a way; just bow your head and say, "Lord Jesus, I want to pray for Tom. I pray that you will strike him with a bolt of lightning for the way he's been treating me this week. In Jesus's name, Amen." But that's not what Jesus has in mind. I believe Jesus wants us to pray that they are blessed, restored, and forgiven.

And from here, it gets even harder. Jesus doesn't stop at telling us to pray for our enemies. As we saw in the last chapter, He also commands us to do good to them. It is one thing to pray for my enemies in private when they don't see it, and I can still give them the stink-eye in person. But how do I do good to my enemies without them feeling like they are being rewarded for their bad behavior? It's almost like Jesus expects me to love these irritating people while they are mistreating me.

Take a minute to picture that person, the one that makes your life so hard, the one that when you replay the conversations in your mind, you can get angry at weeks or months after the issue occurred. Do you see their face? Now, picture yourself making them a plate of cookies, the good ones—with your grandma's recipe and only the best ingredients. Then imagine knocking on their front door or walking into their office with that plate full of love and delivering it in genuineness. Friends, this is getting serious.

But even then, Jesus still isn't finished. In case we aren't catching on, Jesus adds something else to our praying and doing good to our enemies: He says to lend to them without expecting to be repaid. What? This is too much. Imagine a world where our enemies can ask things of us, and we are not only to give to them, but we are not to expect those things ever to be returned. Think of the person who borrows your money, tools, or gas for the lawn mower, these practical everyday things, Jesus says to give them and don't expect them to come back. This applies not only to your friends or your loving family, but to your enemies. Friends, *agape* love requires care on a level that many of us aren't accustomed to giving to the people close to us, much less our enemies. But that is what Jesus is calling us to do.

Now, someone might be asking the reasonable question, "Why did we have to change from the Old Testament approach where people got what they deserved? If an eye for an eye and a tooth for a tooth was good enough for God in the Old Testament, then it's good enough for me."

First, we better consider if we really want to live that way. It is one thing to give cold, hard justice, but what about being on the receiving end? Imagine sitting at an early morning soccer game, families lined up watching their kids out there on the field giving their best, you with your coffee, the dew still wet on the grass, sitting around chit-chatting. Then, suddenly, your little son jumps up to head the soccer ball but instead takes out a tooth of an opposing player. Imagine an economy where your son must walk out to the center of the field, and his tooth is extracted as repayment before the game restarts. If this is how we lived, we might all start to look like the walking dead.

Second, if we study the Old Testament, we might be surprised to discover how God expected His people to live with their enemies back then. Jesus's Sermon on the Mount was not the first time God instructed us to show kindness to our enemies. Proverbs 25:21 says, "If your enemy is hungry, give him food to eat; if he is thirsty, give him water to drink." Exodus 23:4-5 NLT instructs, "If you come upon your enemy's ox or donkey that has strayed away, take it back to its owner. If you see that the donkey of someone who hates you has collapsed under its load, do not walk by. Instead, stop and help."

Now might be a great time to try and answer the question of why? Why should we love our enemies to begin with? Let's go back to Jesus's words in Luke 6:35, where He directly answers this question: "Then your reward will be great, and you will be children of the Most High, because he is kind to the ungrateful and wicked."

Jesus continues in verses 36-38, "Be merciful, just as your Father is merciful. Do not judge, and you will not be judged. Do not condemn, and you will not be condemned. Forgive, and you will be forgiven. Give, and it will be given to you. A good measure, pressed down, shaken together and running over, will be poured into your lap. For with the measure you use, it will be measured to you." This is an amazing promise. If I refuse to judge and condemn my enemies and instead forgive and bless, God will do the same for me. When we love those who have hurt us, God sees that love in action and responds with an overwhelming blessing on our behalf.

How will that blessing be measured out in my life? Listen again: "Good measure, pressed down, shaken together, running over and pouring into your lap." And just what is this reward poured out in great measure? Friends, that reward is grace— wonderful, unmerited, undeserved, and amazing grace.

When we stare down at our enemies, with bitterness seeping into our hearts, frustrated and angry, pondering how we can get even, Jesus gently whispers this question: "Are you sure you want only justice for your enemies? Is that how I responded to you?"

James 4:4 warns us that when we are friends with the world, we become enemies of God, and all of us have, at some point, fallen in love with the world and earned this title of "enemy of God." In Romans 6:23, Paul reminds us, "The wages of sin is death." As sinners and enemies of God, we deserve punishment and death.

Do you remember the moment when God's light shone down into your heart, and it became terribly evident to you just how dark and sinful your life really was? I can still remember the helpless feeling of guilt and shame in my own life when my past life played in front of me like some never-ending R-rated movie. As I faced the reality of my heart's depravity that I was, in fact, an enemy of the Creator, did I, for a moment, cry out to Him for justice? No. When I stood before a Holy God, guilty and condemned, my cry was not for justice but for mercy, unearned forgiveness, and grace.

If God so richly responded to my guilt and yours with unmerited overflowing grace, then as His children, shouldn't we respond the same way to our enemies? Remember, Jesus not only did nice things for His enemies, He died for them. Romans 5:10-11 NLT explains, "For since our friendship with God was restored by the death of his Son while we were still his enemies, we will certainly be saved through the life of his Son. So now we can rejoice in our wonderful new relationship with God because our Lord Jesus Christ has made us friends of God."

The greatest ever act of injustice happened when the sinless Son of God was killed, murdered wrongly on a cross for a people who didn't deserve it at all; and yet at that moment, the greatest act of injustice became the most wonderful act of redemption. When Jesus is commanding us to love our enemies, He is asking us to love the world with the *agape* love He modeled for us, that same undeserved love He poured out on us. He is inviting us to join Him in His mission of redemption.

Read: Matthew 5:46-48, John 13:34-35, I John 4:7-12

Reflect: What practical step can I take today to love my enemies?

Pray: Jesus, thank You for dying for me when I was Your enemy. Thank You for the love You have for my enemies. Teach me to love them with that same undeserved and unconditional love.

CHAPTER 42

Pray for Workers

> *For the first time in Matthew, we're getting the sense that the kingdom-is-at-hand work of Jesus isn't just for Jesus but also for his followers to carry out. This is in other words, the first time in Matthew that we get a glimpse of the church.*
> —*Rachel Starr Thomson, "Pray the Lord of the Harvest"*

Jesus often used farming imagery to illustrate lessons He wanted to teach—things like sowing seed, pruning grape vines, building barns, and even pulling weeds. These were all images that the people of His day understood. The rhythm of their lives was based on harvest and planting and praying to the Lord of the harvest to send the rain, to send the sun, and to provide bounty.

Let's look at Matthew 9:

> **"Jesus went through all the towns and villages, teaching in their synagogues, proclaiming the good news of the kingdom and healing every disease and sickness. When he saw the crowds, he had compassion on them, because they were harassed and helpless, like sheep without a shepherd. Then he said to his disciples, 'The harvest is plentiful but the workers are few. Ask the Lord of the harvest, therefore, to send out workers into his harvest field.'"** Matthew 9:35-38

You'll remember Jesus often talked about sheep and described Himself as the Good Shepherd, like the story of the shepherd who left 99 sheep to go after the one lost sheep. When Jesus looked at the lost people around Him, He saw helpless, harassed, wandering sheep who needed a shepherd. But then Jesus changed His analogy, and instead of calling for more shepherds, He called for more laborers in the harvest field.

Some of you probably remember the old hymn "Bringing in the Sheaves." As a kid, I (Todd) grew up singing that song, having no idea what it meant. In fact, I got the words all wrong. I was singing about bringing in the *sheep* because I had seen pictures of Jesus with sheep. Then, I corrected myself and sang with gusto about bringing in the *sheets* because I saw my mom singing as she brought in the sheets off the clothesline! Only years later did I understand this song is about bringing in the *sheaves*.

If you are like me, the concept of bringing in sheaves isn't familiar. In Jesus's time, as they would harvest wheat, they would gather as much as they could in their arms, hold it, and then cut it down with a sickle or a blade. Then, they would tie it together into a sheaf to be gathered and taken into the barn.[56] The Old Testament taught God's people that He provided the harvest, and they should rejoice as they were "bringing in the sheaves" (Psalm 126:6). In Matthew 9, Jesus is making the connection that He is Lord of a spiritual harvest and needs workers to bring in that harvest.

We started this journey of learning to obey all of Christ's commands by looking at the last chapter of Matthew, what we call the "Great Commission." Here, the risen Jesus meets with His disciples on a mountain and sends them out. "Therefore, go and make disciples of all nations, baptizing them in the name of the Father and of the Son and of the Holy Spirit, and teaching them to observe everything I have commanded you" (Matthew 28:19-20).

For many years, I incorrectly thought this only referred to the commissioning of missionaries, like those who, centuries ago, traveled on wooden ships to distant shores, taking their own coffins with them, knowing they might never come back. But now I believe that, as those disciples walked down the mountain that day, they didn't think of themselves as missionaries. They thought of themselves as laborers being sent into the fields. Jesus had taught them again and again that there is a world waiting, fields already planted and growing and ripe to harvest. Now, it was time for them to go and gather it.

In Acts 2, on the day of Pentecost, when the church was born, Jews from nations all over the world were gathered in Jerusalem. The feast of Pentecost was the celebration of the wheat harvest in Israel. Theologians have estimated that maybe a million additional travelers and pilgrims came to Jerusalem during that time to pray to the Lord of the Harvest. Isn't it interesting how, on that very day, the day set apart to ask God for a bountiful harvest was the day the church was born?

Do you remember how the apostles, filled with the Holy Spirit, rushed into the town square and began to preach the first Gospel message? People from all over the world supernaturally heard that message of Jesus spoken in their own language. Three thousand people were baptized on that day alone. I think when the disciples looked out on that massive crowd that day, they saw wheat fields ready to be harvested. At every baptism, they must have thought, with rejoicing: *Another sheaf has been brought into the Kingdom!*

From that day in Jerusalem, the Gospel spread around the world, generation after generation—seeds planted, crops cultivated, and a harvest brought in. You and I are part of that harvest. We are Christ's followers today because someone was faithful in planting the seed of the Gospel. Then someone cultivated it, watered it, and we gave our life to Christ. And now, you and I are all called to go out into that harvest field and gather the harvest.

Some of us will be traditional missionaries who leave the familiar to travel to distant lands. Some of us will go across the street, down the hall, and around the corner. But we are all workers in the field. The emphasis is not so much on *going* as on *doing*. Wherever we are, there's always a harvest ripe for the picking. Wherever our endeavor, whether it is in our family, neighborhood, school, or workplace, we are called on to plant the seed of the Word. Simply put, whoever you are, wherever you're posted, whatever gifts God has given you, you are called to go into the field to intentionally sow, cultivate, and reap.

I've served as a campus minister at Christ in Youth's summer crusades for many years. Last year, I was asked to make an announcement at a morning session inviting students interested in "full-time vocational ministry" to attend a workshop later in the afternoon where I would talk to them about those opportunities. By definition, "full-time vocational ministry" means being trained to be a pastor, youth minister, children's minister, worship minister, or missionary. Even as I made the announcement, I was thinking I'd be lucky to have ten kids show up. I had a sense that there just wasn't that much interest or urgency in this generation to dedicate themselves to full-time ministry. But when the time came, to my surprise, over a hundred teenagers flooded into that room. As I talked and answered questions, there was energy and excitement, and when it was over, a line of students waited patiently to speak with me one-on-one.

I am proud to say that several from my church were included in that group of students. And while we should applaud those who are called into "full-time vocational ministry," we also need to be intentional in encouraging young people who are called to be dentists, engineers, teachers, mechanics, or whatever their field, that they too have a place. They too are a Kingdom worker; it's just a different path.

Jesus also talked about the eternal consequences of the last and final harvest. In Matthew 13, He told a parable about a wealthy man who planted wheat, and in the middle of the night, one of his enemies came in and planted weeds along with the grain. As it was just beginning to come up, the manager of that field went to the owner and said, "Sir, I don't know how this happened. I'm so embarrassed— thick weeds are growing with the wheat. What should I do? Should I pull the weeds out?" The owner said, "No, the roots are not deep enough yet. Everything is still too green. If you pull the weeds up, you'll pull the wheat as well, and you'll lose the whole crop. The enemy has done this to us, so here's what we'll do. We'll wait for harvest time and then separate the wheat from the weeds."

After Jesus's disciples asked for help understanding this parable, Jesus explained:

> The one who sowed the good seed is the Son of Man. The field is the world, and the good seed stands for the people of the kingdom. The weeds are the people of the evil one, and the enemy who sows them is the devil. The harvest is the end of the age, and the harvesters are angels. As the weeds are pulled up and burned in the fire, so it will be at the end of the age. The Son of Man will send out his angels, and they will weed out of his kingdom everything that causes sin and all who do evil. They will throw them into the blazing furnace, where there will be weeping and gnashing of teeth. Then the righteous will shine like the sun in the kingdom of their Father. Whoever has ears, let them hear. (Matthew 13:37-43)

At the end of the age, when our Lord returns, there will be a great harvest representing the true church, all believers from the living and dead, who will shine with the sun's brilliance. But there will be another harvest, described in Revelation 14, a grape harvest. The grapes represent sinful people who will be thrown together into the winepress of God's fury, where they will be trampled. These are the ones Jesus said would be expelled into a place of outer darkness where there is weeping and gnashing of teeth.

Sadly, in recent days, the church has become comfortable and slumbering— not many are going, and not many are harvesting. While we should be a great army, we often look more like the scene you see on the news of a hurricane washing over the shore, and people hunkered down, plywood over their windows, burning candles, just riding out the storm. The church has adopted a storm mentality: It's too dark, it's too bad, it's too evil, it's too overwhelming, it's too impossible, and we should just hunker down and hold on tight until the storm passes and we get to go to Heaven.

But there have been many other challenging times in church history when people stood their ground in the face of great evil. They plunged into the darkness and scattered throughout the world to bring in a great harvest. One of those dark times was in 1940 when Adolph Hitler was sending his Nazi troops all over Europe. Poland, Norway, Denmark, Belgium, the Netherlands, and France had all fallen. Britain stood almost alone in the face of Hitler's onslaught. Night after night, the Nazi bombing brought devastation. On June 18, at 9:00 pm, Winston Churchill made a radio speech that I consider one of the most inspirational speeches in the history of mankind:

> …the Battle of France is over; I expect that the Battle of Britain is about to begin. Upon this battle depends the survival of Christian civilization. Upon it depends our own British life and our long continuity of our constitutions and empire. The whole fury and might of the enemy must very soon be turned on us. Hitler knows that he will have to break us in this Island or lose the war. If we can stand up to him, all Europe may be freed and the life of the world may move forward into broad sunlit uplands. But if we fail then the whole world including the United States, including all that we have known and cared for, will sink into the abyss of a new Dark Age made more sinister and perhaps more protracted by the likes of perverted science. Let us, therefore, brace ourselves to our duty and so bear ourselves that if the British Empire and its Commonwealth last for a thousand years, men will say this was their finest hour.[57]

What will future generations say about us? About you?

This is not the time to shrink back, to be afraid, to be hesitant, or to be unwilling. This is the time to pray fervently, to be greatly used, to be God's people in this place, in this time, with all the energy He's already provided for us. This is our finest hour.

Read: John 4:35-38, Acts 2:38-47, Revelation 14:14-20

Reflect: How am I being used in God's harvest fields?

Pray: Jesus, You taught us to pray for laborers in Your harvest fields. Send laborers. And send me. I know the need is great, and I want to be a part of Your harvest.

CONCLUSION

Keep My Commandments

Over the last 42 chapters, we have walked together through the Gospels and the Book of Revelation, identifying Jesus's commands. It is our hope that as you have studied these commands, they have shaped how you live your life. Remember the truly effective discipleship program we have all been searching for? It is right here, "hidden in plain sight," recorded in the words of Scripture. Let's look one more time at the marching orders Jesus gave to His disciples, charging them to change the world:

> **"Then Jesus came to them and said, 'All authority in heaven and on earth has been given to me. Therefore, go and make disciples of all nations, baptizing them in the name of the Father and of the Son and of the Holy Spirit, teaching them to obey everything I have commanded you. And surely, I am with you always, to the very end of the age.'"**
> **Matthew 28:18-20**

When the church was launched in Acts 2, people were being saved every day. What was the secret? Luke reveals the simple discipleship program of the early church: They were devoted to the apostles' doctrine—the commands of Jesus. The disciples simply taught the early church all that Jesus had taught them!

Let's go one more time to the upper room. In these last hours with His disciples, Jesus washes their feet and institutes the Lord's Supper. Then Jesus gave His last training session to these men who had walked with Him for three-and-a-half years. Here we find one of the commands that Jesus saved to the very end:

> **"If you love me, keep my commands." John 14:15**

That night Jesus would reiterate this theme multiple times:

"Whoever has my commands and keeps them is the one who loves me. The one who loves me will be loved by my Father, and I too will love them and show myself to them" (John 14:21).

"Anyone who loves me will obey my teaching. My Father will love them, and we will come to them and make our home with them. Anyone who does not love me will not obey my teaching. These words you hear are not my own; they belong to the Father who sent me" (John 14:23-24).

"If you keep my commands, you will remain in my love, just as I have kept my Father's commands and remain in his love" (John 15:10).

"You are my friends if you do what I command" (John 15:14).

Do you really love Jesus? If you really want to know the answer to that question, you have to ask yourself another question: Do I keep His commands? See, that's the proof; that's what Jesus was trying to tell His disciples. The litmus test for loving Jesus isn't how religious you are, how often you go to church, how much you give, what you look like, or how pious you seem. What determines whether we truly love Jesus is whether or not we keep His commands.

When Jesus spoke these words in the upper room, it was not a new concept to His disciples. It had been instilled in them over and over from childhood. It was Bible 101 for Hebrew children. Listen to these words found in the book of Exodus right between commandments number five and six, describing God, "showing love to a thousand generations of those who love me and keep my commandments" (Exodus 20:6).

Later, after forty years of wandering in the desert, with the Promised Land finally in sight, Moses gathered all of Israel together and recited the Law of God from Mount Horeb. He instructs them to observe God's commands and teach them to their children. He continues with these well-known words:

> Hear, O Israel: The Lord our God, the Lord is one. Love the Lord your God with all your heart and with all your soul and with all your strength. These commandments that I give you today are to be on your hearts. Impress them on your children. Talk about them when you sit at home and when you walk along the road, when you lie down and when you get up. Tie them as symbols on your hands and bind them on your foreheads.

> Write them on the doorframes of your houses and on your gates. (Deuteronomy 6:4-9)

When Peter preached that first message at Pentecost, the people who heard were cut to the heart and asked what they should do. Peter told them, "Repent and be baptized every one of you in the name of Jesus Christ for the forgiveness of your sins. And you will receive the gift of the Holy Spirit. This promise is for you and your children and for all who are far off—for all whom the Lord our God will call" (Acts 2:38). He was telling them and telling us, salvation is for you, but it is also available to your children, to the next generation, and a thousand generations afterward. It is for all who obey God's commands.

The real secret of an effective discipleship program goes beyond just obeying God's commands. That is just the start. We have to pass down His commands from generation to generation. What is the most effective discipleship program in the history of the world? Parents teaching their children the commands of God. Not a priest, not a preacher, not a Sunday school teacher, but moms and dads teaching their children the commands of God.

When I (Todd) became a dad, someone gave me a book that changed my life, *The Effective Father* by Gordan MacDonald. In his premise to the first chapter, he shares this story that set the tone for the book:

> When George Yeager took his three sons and an elderly grandfather out on the Atlantic Ocean for a fishing trip, he had no premonition of the horror he would face in a matter of hours. Before he would step on the shore again, Yeager would watch each son and then his father die. Victims of exhaustion and lungs filled with water.
>
> The boat's engine had stalled in the late afternoon while increasing winds whipped the sea into great rolling waves. The boat rolled helplessly in the water and then began to list dangerously. When it became apparent that they were sinking, the five Yeager men put on the life vests and tied themselves together with a rope and slipped into the water. It was 6:30 PM when the sinking craft disappeared, and the swimmers set out to work their way toward shore.
>
> Six-foot waves and a strong current made the swimming almost impossible. First one boy and then another and another swallowed too much water; helpless, George Yeager watched his sons

and then his father die. Eight hours later he staggered onto the shore still pulling the rope that bound the bodies of the other four to him.

"I realized they were all dead. My three boys and my dad. But I guess I didn't want to accept it, so I just kept swimming all through the night," he told the reporters. "My youngest boy, Clifford, was the first to go, I had always taught our children not to fear death because it meant being with Jesus and before he died, I heard him through the storm say, 'I'd rather be with Jesus than go on fighting.'" [58]

What a father! Did you notice what he said to the reporters? "I had always taught our children . . ."

Parents, we've spent a lot of time teaching our children many things. We taught them to walk, use utensils at the table, and ride a bike. Maybe we've taught them to fish, play sports, excel at math and science, how to play an instrument or change a tire. We've worked hard to teach them some things about life that really matter. And yet, when it comes to teaching them the commands of Jesus, we may have fallen short. Listen, when I look back on my time as a father, I am heartbroken about all the opportunities that I missed. As I have gone through this study, I've seen how much more intentional I could have been along the way.

Mom and Dad, may I give you some real practical advice? Bring your children to church. Don't leave it up to them. Get involved. Ask them what they've learned as you're riding home from church. As you sit down for dinner, make it a practice to talk to them about God. Don't relegate spiritual discussions and prayer to something that only happens on Sundays. Play Christian music in your home. Make the holidays Christ-centered. And at just the right time in your child's life, ask them if they are ready to give their life to Christ. When they make that decision, talk to them about committing their lives to Jesus through baptism.

Make sure you are living out Jesus's commands in front of them. Please, don't claim to follow Jesus and live like you don't. May this be your theme: "Let the message of Christ dwell among you richly as you teach and admonish one another with all wisdom through singing psalms, hymns and songs from the Spirit, singing to God with gratitude in your hearts. In whatever you do whether in word or deed, do it all in the name of the Lord Jesus, giving thanks to God the Father through him" (Colossians 3:16-18).

Parents or not, to our own children or the children around us, all of us have a role in passing down Jesus's commands from one generation to another. Our children are facing many stormy crises. In the darkest hour of their lives, the only thing they have left is what we've taught them about Jesus.

Do you want to be a part of the most effective discipleship strategy of all time? Love Jesus. Obey His commands. Share His love with those around you. And pass on Christ's commands to the next generation.

Endnotes

1. Lockshin, Shoshanna. "What Is a Mikveh?" *My Jewish Learning.* 21 Nov. 2022. www.myjewishlearning.com/article/the-mikveh/

2. Washer, Paul. "Some Of Paul Washer's 27 Best Sermons." https://www.puritandownloads.com/swrb/news/117/Some-of-Paul-Washer%27s-Best-Free-MP3-Sermons.html

3. Colson, Chuck. *Kingdoms in Conflict.* Zondervan, 1987. 202-3.

4. Elliot, Elizabeth. *Shadow of the Almighty.* Hendrickson Publishing, 2008.

5. Miller, Calvin. *quotefancy.* https://quotefancy.com/quote/1713655/Calvin-Miller-A-passion-to-obey-Christ-is-born-out-of-our-relationship-with-him-The-more

6. *Strong's Concordance* #4576, "Adore, adoration."

7. *Strong's Concordance* # 4352, "*Proskuneo.*"

8. *Dictionary.com>slang dictionary.* 27 August 2018. https://www.dictionary.com/e/slang/come-to-jesus/#:~:text=Just%20as%20finding%20Jesus%20is,i.e.%2C%20changing%20one's%20ways).

9. Eberstadt, Mary. *It's Dangerous to Believe: Religious Freedom and Its Enemies.* Harper Collins. 2016.

10. "7 Active Listening Techniques for Better Communication." https://www.verywellmind.com/what-is-active-listening-3024343.

11. *brainyquote.com.* https://www.brainyquote.com/quotes/larry_king_130681.

12. Palmer, Michael R. "The Discipline of Secrecy." The Foundry Community. 28 March 2022. https://www.thefoundrycommunity.com/the-discipline-of-secrecy/#:~:text=The%20Discipline%20of,March%2028%2C%202022 .

13. Twain, Mark. *brainyquotes.com.* https://www.brainyquote.com/quotes/mark_twain_153875#:~:text=It%20ain%27t%20those,Mark%20Twain.

¹⁴ Piper, John. *What Jesus Demands from the World*. Wheaton, Illinois: Crossway, 2006. 92.

¹⁵ Singh, Abhishek, Executive Director of the Planetary Development Institute. "Unity of Religions: Certainly no Confusion." 04 February 2018. http://planetaryproject.com/.

¹⁶ *Strong's Concordance*. # 75 "*agónizomai,* strive to enter."

¹⁷ "Porn Profits: Corporate America's Secret." *abcnews.go.com*. 27 January 2003.

¹⁸ Franklin, Benjamin. *The Writings of Benjamin Franklin, Vol. X* (1789-1790). Ed. Jared Sparks. Macmillan, 1856. 410.

¹⁹ Twain, Mark. *BrainyQuotes.com*. https://www.brainyquote.com/quotes/mark_twain_163134#:~:text=What%20is%20the,Mark%20Twain

²⁰ Roberts, Mark D. "Steadfastness of Hope, Part 2". Fuller De Pree Center, 30 May 2022. https://depree.org/life-for-leaders/steadfastness-of-hope-part-2/#:~:text=If%20you%20look%20hupomone%20up,Thessalonian%20Christians%20had%20been%20demonstrating

²¹ H, Jim. "Ernest Shackleton – Surviving Antarctica". *HistoricMysteries.com*. 30 May 2015. https://www.historicmysteries.com/history/ernest-shackleton/1146/#:~:text=HISTORY-,Ernest%20Shackleton%20%E2%80%93%20Surviving%20Antartica,by%20Jim%20H%20May%2030%2C%202015,-0

²² Isaacs, Stan. "Bud's Olympiads Are Worth Their Weight in Gold." *Newsday*. 5 November 1991: 109.

²³ Watkins, Julian Lewis. *The 100 Greatest Advertisements 1852-1958: Who Wrote Them and What They Did*. Mineola: Dover Publications, 1949. 1.

²⁴ Rice, Wayne. *Hot Illustrations for Youth Talks*. Youth Specialties Books, Zondervan, 1993.

²⁵ *merriam-webster.com*. "Nincompoop."

²⁶ "Count the Crimes on the Federal Law Books. Then Cut Them." *heritage.org*. 24 June 2020.

(This piece originally appeared in *The Daily Signal*).

²⁷ Ten Boom, Corrie. "On Forgiving Your Enemies," from *The Hiding Place. lexionarycentral*.com. http://www.lectionarycentral.com/trinity22/Boom.html

²⁸ Ditto.

29 Ditto.

30 Ditto.

31 Williamson, Marianne. *BrainyQuote.com*. https://www.brainyquote.com/quotes/marianne_williamson_635346#:~:text=Unforgiveness%20is%20like,Marianne%20Williamson.

32 Greene, Emily Harris. "Joe and Amy: A Story of Reconciliation." *prisonfellowship.org*.

33 Memmott, Mark. "What A Rush! California Couple Finds Gold Coins Worth $10M." 26 Feb. 2014. https://www.npr.org/.

34 *dictionary.com*. "covetousness."

35 "Bits and Pieces." November 1991. -http://www.bible.org/illus/g/g-83.htm].

36 Accelus. "What Is the Difference Between Persist and Determination?" *acceluspartners.com*. https://acceluspartners.com/what-is-the-difference-between-determination-and-persistence/.

37 Graham, Billy. "Ten Quotes from Billy Graham On Prayer." The Billy Graham Library. 5 March 2019. https://billygrahamlibrary.org/blog-10-quotes-from-billy-graham-on-prayer/#:~:text=10%20Quotes%20from%20Billy%20Graham%20on%20Prayer

38 Sampson, John. "Who Was Praying for Me Tuesday Night?" *effectualgrace.com*. 12 August 2012. https://effectualgrace.com/2012/08/15/who-was-praying-for-me-tuesday-night/#:~:text=%E2%80%98Who%20Was%20Praying%20for%20Me%20Tuesday%20Night%3F%E2%80%99.

39 Ditto.

40 "Horatio Gates Spafford - The story behind the hymn 'It is well with my soul.'" *bethelripon.com*. December 2018. https://www.bethelripon.com/life-stories/horatio-gates-spafford#:~:text=Horatio%20Gates%20Spafford%2D%20The%20story%20behind%20the%20hymn%20%22It%20is%20well%20with%20my%20soul%22.

41 Spafford, Horatio Gates. "It Is Well." *Hymnal.net*. https://www.hymnal.net/en/hymn/h/341#:~:text=Search-,It%20is%20well,-Audio%20Player.

42 Luther, Martin. *azquotes.com* https://www.azquotes.com/quote/576079#:~:text=work%20it%20is...-,%5BChrist%27s%5D%20mission%20and%20work%20it%20is%20to%20help%20against%20sin%20and,Martin%20Luther,-Favorite.

43 Ryle, J. C. *azquotes.com.* https://www.azquotes.com/quote/917917#:~:text=No%20doubt%20a%20man%20may%20be%20saved,obey%20Christ%20and%20attend%20the%20Lord%27s%20Table.

44 Shakespeare, William. *brainyquote.com.* https://www.brainyquote.com/quotes/william_shakespeare_155088#:~:text=How%20far%20that,William%20Shakespeare.

45 "Salt Of the Earth." *Worth Your Salt.* https://www.saltoftheearth.com.au/worth-your-salt/#:~:text=WORTH%20YOUR%20SALT-,Worth%20Your%20Salt,-POSTED%20IN%3A.

46 *Pinterst.com>William Tyndale* https://www.pinterest.com/pin/william-tyndale--362047257538636403/#:~:text=%E2%80%9CThe%20Church%20is%20the%20one%20institution%20that%20exists%20for%20those%20outside%20it.%E2%80%9D%20%E2%80%93%20William%20Tyndale%20Actsof2020vision.com.

47 Hines, Abijah. "Being Fed in School Is a Right, not a Privilege." *The Current.* 19 Jan. 2023. https://wmcurrent.com/.

48 Baucham, Voddie. "Reformed Christian Quotes." 8 June 2022. https://www.facebook.com/Reformed.Christian.quote?__tn__=-UC*F.

49 Douglass, Frederick. *Narrative of the Life of Frederick Douglass, an American Slave.* 1818-1895. Electronic Edition.

50 Douglass, Frederick. "The Anna Murray and Frederick Douglass Family Letter 'To My Old Master, Thomas Auld.'" *Struggles For Liberty.* https://digital.nls.uk/learning/struggles-for-liberty/themes/the-anna-murray-and-frederick-douglass-family/letter-to-my-old-master-thomas-auld/#:~:text=The%20Anna%20Murray,Master%2C%20Thomas%20Auld%27.

51 Ironsides, Henry. *Illustrations of Bible Truth.* https://www.sermonillustrations.com/a-z/b/bishop.htm.

52 *Strong's Concordance* # 2919 *krinó.*

53 Garofalo, Michael. Produced for *Morning Edition.* https://www.npr.org/2008/03/28/89164759/a-victim-treats-his-mugger-right.

54 Kelly, Walt, artist. "Earth Day Illustration." 1970.

55 *Strong's Concordance* #26, *Agape.*

56 Verret, Bethany. "Why Do We Sing about 'Bringing in the Sheaves'"? Bible Study Tools. 6 August 2021. https://www.biblestudytools.com/bible-study/topical-studies/why-do-we-sing-about-bringing-in-the-sheaves.html#:~:text=Login-,Why%20Do%20We%20

Sing%20about%20%E2%80%9CBringing%20in%20the%20 Sheaves%E2%80%9D%3F,-Bethany%20Verrett

[57] Churchill, Winston. "The Finest Hour Speech." History of the Net. https://www.historyonthenet.com/finest-hour-speech#:~:text= Down%20Communist%20Spies-,The%20Finest%20Hour%20 Speech,-History%20%C2%BB%20World

[58] MacDonald, Gordon. *The Effective Father.* Tyndale House Publishers, 1977.

Find free church and small group resources at commandsofchrist.info.

www.ingramcontent.com/pod-product-compliance
Lightning Source LLC
Chambersburg PA
CBHW021148160426
43194CB00007B/730